So Much
Sky

Essays on the fun and folly of living in the country

Karen Weir-Jimerson

Publisher
Studio G
13673 R Avenue
Woodward, IA 50276
www.studiogonline.com

Acknowledgment is made to *Country Home* magazine, in which the following columns were originally published in a slightly different form: "A Close Shave," "Courting the Purple Martin," "Spring Lambing," "May Flowers," "The Color of Calm," "A Kitten Caper," "Horse Sense," "Old Dog, Timeless Tricks," "Eating Close to Home," "Hold Your Horses," "Backyard Archeology," "Finding the Elusive Fungi," "A Little Bird Told Me," "Gliding into Summer," "Summer Docking," "Something Afowl," "Blowing in the Wind," "I Love a Parade," "When the Cats Are Away...," "Water Garden Wonders," "Off to Auction," "Planting a Legacy," "Fence Defense," "Airstream Dreams," "Traveling Time and Distance," "Fair Game," "In the Heart of the Country," "Mice Capades," "Driving Miss Daisy," "Pressing Matters," "They Call It Puppy Love," "Planting Bulbs," "Autumn Hitchhiking," "Straight from the Horse's Mouth," "Keeping the Home Fires Burning," "Picking the Perfect Pumpkin," "Tornado Season," "Horse Play," "Latitudinal Longings," "Frost Takes No Prisoners," "Chiming In," "Found Objects," "Short but Fulfilling Winter Days," "Straw into Gold," "Closet Confessions," "Faux, Faux, Faux...Merry Christmas," "Every Picture Tells a Story," "Tracking Movements," "Life of Riley," "Star Power," and "Regarding Winter."

Acknowledgment is made to *Country Almanac* magazine, in which the following columns were originally published in a slightly different form: "The Chicks Are in the Mail," "One Potato, Two Potato," and "Snow Day!"

Acknowledgment is made to *Horticulture* magazine, in which "Frost Takes No Prisoners" was originally published in a slightly different form.

Photos: Graham Jimerson
Design: Ryan Alexander

Library of Congress Cataloguing-in-Publication Data
Weir-Jimerson, Karen.
So Much Sky / by Karen Weir-Jimerson ; illustrations by Anna Bongiovanni
ISBN-13: 978-1463502430
ISBN-10: 1463502435

Printed in the United States

For Doug, Tristan, and Graham

Thanks go to my husband, Doug,
with whom I have consulted (and at whom I have poked fun)
in this book. Our journey together in this life has made this book
possible. And to my sons, Tristan and Graham, whose wonder
and humor informed many of the stories here.

I'd also like to gratefully acknowledge
County Home magazine, a publication
of Meredith Corporation, for permission
to reprint my "Slow Lane" columns,
published in that magazine from 2003 to 2009.

Contents

Introduction

I may have grown up in town, but I'm a country girl now. On three acres in rural Iowa, I've experienced about everything the country has to offer—serene summer days with an orchestra of happy crickets, to towering thunderstorms that produced winds strong enough to flatten our windbreak and grove. But for me, my husband Doug, and sons Tristan and Graham, living in the country has been both a journey and a destination.

Compared to the farms around us, our 3-acre plot is small potatoes. But on this varied piece of ground we've created several large gardens, renovated outdated farm buildings into new, useful structures, and gathered a menagerie of beasts both great and small. Our 20th-century farmhouse has blossomed under many home improvement projects. The house didn't even have a bathroom until 1955, but now boasts three.

Living in the country allows us to indulge in our love of animals. We started out with the requisite dogs and cats. Poultry followed—what farm is complete without a crowing rooster and a bevy of fat hens scratching about?

Then we added "shepherd" to our list of farm skills. We started out with Jacob sheep, a rare English breed that is spotted black and white and has four horns. You can understand the shocked look on the shearer's face when our multi-horned ram walked out of the barn... We've raised several sheep breeds: Cheviots, Romney, and Dorsets. Our current flock is small: six Katahdins, a sheep bred in Maine that requires neither shearing nor docking (tail removal). Katahdins are the lazy shepherd's dream sheep. They are vigilant groundskeepers, keeping the pasture grazed with precision.

As we found success with one species, we wanted more. Each addition got larger. We added three miniature donkeys, Riley, Cisco, and Peso, to the farm. Although they don't fit the mold of the classic farm animal (they don't produce eggs, wool, meat, or do work of any kind) the donkeys are the comedians of the farm and are as friendly and engaging as our dogs. Of course, then we had to try horses and now own three—a quarter horse for riding and a matched pair of small draft horses for driving.

Sharing our land with these animals can be both calming and fearsome. On a good day, you'll find all the animals milling about calmly—a peaceable kingdom in the pasture. Other days, they spend their spare time searching for loose spots in the fence (and finding them). Neighbors call with news that our flock has escaped and we head out the door with our Border collies, who bring them back to the farm the same way that dogs have moved sheep for centuries—with the purpose and skill that has been learned and passed on through their breeding.

My favorite act of the day is feeding the horses, donkeys, and sheep in the morning and evening. Their gentle greetings when I step into the farm yard, their bumps and nudges as I grain and hay them, and the methodical sounds of chewing, are so consistent and lulling that even on the chilliest of days I return to the house warmed by this simple exchange.

This book gets its title from a comment made by my husband's stepmother Mary. On her first visit to the farm, after spending a whole lifetime living in Brookyln, New York, she got out of the car, cowered a bit and said, "Douglas, you have so much sky here." And she was right.

These essays represent the fun, fantasy, and folly of living in the country on a small farmstead. Each season brings with it a group of activities that defines the year on the farm—and in many cases delineates the cycle of life.

spring

A Close Shave

In late spring, after our small flock of Dorset sheep have given birth to their lambs, we have our annual sheep shearing. Although the sheep most likely view this day as ten minutes of indignity followed by a chilly couple of weeks with a too-short coat, our family looks forward to sheep shearing as a time to get together with friends and to marvel at these benign wool factories on hooves.

Not being handy with scissors, we hire a local sheep shearer who arrives in his weathered pickup truck on a cool Saturday morning in March with his barbering tools sharpened and ready to roll. The shearer is in hot demand this time of year, and his calendar is booked with stops to small farms like ours with a handful of sheep in need of a spring clip. If there's been a rain the sheep will be too wet to shear, and we'll have to reschedule. But as it happens this day, we have clear skies and a cold spring morning that's perfect for shearing.

As parents and kids gather around the barn entrance making hair-cutting jokes, the shearer sets to work. He lays down a tarp on the cool concrete barn floor, plugs in his electric shears, and waits expectantly for the first customer. Earlier that morning, my husband Doug, with the help of our Border collie, Rose, had moved the sheep into a stall in the barn where they stomped their hooves and bleated with impatience at being gathered so close together.

It's a woolly mammoth of a ram who is the first to be sheared. He's led into the shearing area and looks around nervously at the visitors. With a swiftness that elicits impressed "ahhs" from the crowd, and a quick, surprised "bahhh" from the ram, the shearer whips the ram over onto his backside, rendering him totally helpless. Seated on a tarp with his legs sticking straight out, the ram couldn't look more shocked. He struggles for a moment, can't get a foothold, and then relaxes. The shearer revs up his electric blades.

With deft swipes, the shearer releases the ram from his woolly covering. Each stroke yields a thick, curled mass that rolls off sideways revealing the pink skin beneath. The wool is dark and muddy on the outside where it's been exposed to the elements, but underneath, close to the skin, the fleece is golden yellow. The ram seems to get smaller with each pass of the blades. The shearer balances the ram's body with one hand, and gently turns him as he works. Most of the ram's wool comes off like a giant overcoat. I catch myself looking for a zipper.

The kids stand open-mouthed as the ram emerges from the barn. It's as though he's been born again—he's all legs and covered with short nappy new wool. He runs stiffly out into the pasture, "bahhing" his displeasure. Left behind him on the floor is a bale of golden curled fleece. We pull off the dirtiest of the wool and discard it, then pack the clean fleece into a large plastic bag. The shearer looks up for the next customer. And thus the morning passes.

Each newly shorn sheep joins the previously-shaved in the barnyard, along with bawling lambs who don't recognize their moms without all their fluff. The barnyard fills with slim, shorn sheep. When the last ewe is finished, the shearer stands up straight, bends slightly backward to unhinge his back from hours of stooped work, and starts packing up. He has more farms to visit today, more sheep to shear. Before he bags up the last of the golden wool (which he sells to the local wool buyer), the children fill up plastic bags with lanolin-rich wool for school show-and-tells. We all walk away from the barn, rubbing our hands with the thick oiliness that the wool has left behind.

Then we head for the house, where we stand in the kitchen drinking coffee and juice and munching down donuts and rolls—trying to warm up. Outside in the barnyard, the sheep are grazing happily on new spring grass, having already forgotten their morning's close shave.

Courting the Purple Martin

Purple martins—those shapely, iridescent members of the swallow family—are the coveted summer tenants of backyard naturalists all across North America, from Alabama to Canada. Reputed to eat their weight in annoying flying insects each day all summer, they soar through the skies like Cirque du Soleil artists as they feed.

Shortly after Doug bought the turn-of-the-century farmhouse where our family now lives, he decided to welcome purple martins to our yard by erecting a veritable purple martin mansion overlooking our garden seating area. We envisioned these graceful flyers swooping dramatically over the garden, devouring beakfuls of pesky bugs with each acrobatic turn. We would sit peacefully under this sky show, drinking chilled glasses of wine, every once in awhile toasting our St.-Francis-of-Assisi-like rapport with birds. Life would be good.

With high expectations and some background research on the housing requirements of martins, we erected our purple martin house, a white metal building with 12 comfy nesting compartments. Outside each nesting hole was a slim chrome railing, like a tiny modern veranda. I could easily envision noisy groups of martins flying in and out of this abode, making it their home for years and years.

We sank the steel pole into the ground, pulled the birdhouse up the pole with a rope (much like raising a flag) to about 15 feet in the air, and stood back to admire its bright whiteness against the cloudless blue sky. We stood there, faces upturned, eagerly scanning the heavens for our first pair of purple martins to arrive. After 10 minutes, and now with painful cricks in our necks, we returned indoors to give our inevitable first family of martins a little privacy. We watched for their arrival from our family room window with binoculars. We scanned the skies for martins from our front and back porches. But, alas, the martins never came that year.

Nor did they come for the next 18 years, even though we erected a companion house—we now had room for 24 pairs of purple martins. What were we doing wrong? As real estate brokers say, home selection is based on three things: location, location, location. Driving around our town, we could see many happy families of purple martins living it up in yards very similar to ours. What were we lacking? I did more avian research and determined that our birdhouses were positioned correctly (out of the way of structures and trees, in order to give the martins an open place to fly and feed, the right height, dimensions, and type of construction). But each fall, feeling thoroughly snubbed, we lowered our virgin houses, sealed up the nesting holes for the winter, and hoped for martins to come the following spring.

Finally, in our 19th year of trying to win the hearts and minds of purple martins, we saw our first "scout" martin. In the early spring, flocks of purple martins leave their winter residences in South America, and wing their way northward in search of summer nesting sites. The martin scouts fly ahead of the rest of the flock and locate summer homes. These amazing birds have strong "site fidelity," which means they return to nest in the same house (sometimes even the same nesting hole) each year. We were hoping for a scout in search of new real estate.

It was a warm April day when we spotted a lone purple martin scout circling around the twin houses over our garden. But then, from out of nowhere, a muddy brown house sparrow swooped down and attacked the travel-weary martin. To our dismay, we discovered that house sparrows had moved into our martin condos and were now doing their best to muscle out the competition. We ran outside, lowered the houses, and started tearing out the sparrow nests.

"What are you *doing*?" my son Tristan incredulously asked.

"Evicting sparrows," I said, as I tossed the nests onto the ground.

"Why?" he asked.

"To attract purple martins," I said, as I flung more nesting material cavalierly over the fence.

"Do you think that after the martins see you destroying bird nests they'll really want to move right in?" he said sarcastically.

I thought to myself, "What a wise and wise-cracking boy I've raised."

"Good point," I said, as I emptied out the last of the squatters' nests and raised the houses back up the poles.

Luckily, my heartless act of nest busting went unheeded by all. Although the sparrows attacked the martins (and me, as I ripped up their nesting handiwork), all this violence wasn't enough to deter the martin scout who returned the next day with an entourage of "martinettes" who happily moved into one of the houses, and immediately started assembling nests. Ever the opportunists, the house sparrows quickly moved back into the other martin house.

We now have a sky-high neighborhood of rival birds who, every once in awhile, mix it up in the airspace over the garden—sort of our own aerial *West Side Story*. Not the peaceful scene I'd hoped for, but I'll take what I can get.

At last we have martins! We are satisfied with our growing group, and at last they are satisfied with us. They've come back two years in a row now, so I think we can finally say that we are solidly FOPM (Friends Of Purple Martins).

Spring Lambing

Every spring on our farm we enjoy the same ritual of renewal—spring lambing. Our small flock of sheep delivers single lambs and sometimes twins over a period of a couple weeks—mostly with amazing skill and independence. Depending on the weather and the ewes' mothering abilities, lambing can go smoothly—or it can be a comedy of errors, as it was last spring.

The first error was ours, Doug's and mine. We neglected to write down the date that we put the ram in to breed the ewes. Instead, we trusted our ever-porous memories to recall that it would be just five months from that day that our ewes would start delivering lambs. But somehow this date was forgotten or mixed up with other important farm dates (when to worm the horses, or the date our mail-order chicks would arrive), so when the first lamb was born in April, no one was there to greet it. This general lack of interest extended to the first-time mom, who unceremoniously delivered her little bundle of wool onto the muddy ground, then promptly walked away without so much as a backward glance.

When a ewe isn't interested in mothering her lamb your job as a shepherd is to place the two together in a barn stall, and do a little matchmaking. One person quiets the mother, while another person positions the lamb at teat's edge and urges it to suckle. Usually this little bonding exercise causes the mother to remember what she's supposed to do and, at the same time, teaches the new lamb where to find milk. In our experience, this bonding does take place about 80 percent of the time. And if the matchmaking doesn't work, you get a bottle lamb. That spring we had three bottle lambs—an unusually large number.

Bottle lambs are just what they sound like—lambs that feed from a bottle every couple of hours. Luckily for all involved, there is a commercial lamb formula that mixes up just like baby formula. The powdered formula dissolves in warm water and creates a creamy mixture that smells like a milkshake. To feed the lambs, we pour the formula into a plastic pop bottle retrofitted with a bright red nipple designed just for them.

We creatively named our needy wards Lamby, Lamby, and Lamby. They all came running when we called their communal name, and swarmed around, head-butting us in the knees, looking for a mouthful of milk. (Lambs butt at the mother's teat in order to release milk.)

They were fun to feed. In the first couple of weeks, the orphaned lambs were easy to handle and vigorously nursed their formula from repurposed Mountain Dew bottles. Tristan and Graham eagerly helped out, often arguing over who would get to feed the lambs first. But after several days of round-the-clock feedings, the Lamby trio were more pests than pets to the kids, which meant that full nursing honors fell to Doug and me.

Feeding three greedy bottle lambs at the same time is not an easy task. As you might guess, patience is not a virtue among hungry livestock. After much trial and error (and many bottles knocked onto the muddy ground), I devised a position that allowed me to become a three-lamb feeding station: I wedged a bottle between my knees and held one bottle in each hand. Voila! Then all I had to do was brace myself for the onslaught of hungry lambs.

And eat they did! About the time my back felt like it was never going to unlock from that stooped position, I heard the telltale sounds that signaled a finished bottle. As I slowly stood up, I listened to my vertebrae crack as I regained my full height. Feeding time was over for another couple of hours.

The Lambys grew bigger and bolder, and I must admit that coming into the barnyard and being mobbed by these boisterous woolly babes was curiously fun. One of the Lambys followed me everywhere I went with the devotion and dedication of a dog. One day I trekked out to the end of the pasture to make sure the fence was still standing after a hard spring rain, and this lovable Lamby hiked with me, even crossing a precarious plank footbridge over the creek. Little Lamby followed me into the yard, into the barn and, no doubt, would have come into the house for tea had I invited her.

During the day the trio of Lambys stood in the farmyard, staring longingly through the fence at the house. Upon seeing any human in the yard, the Lambys would crowd around the gate, bawling in unison. All the while the rest of the sheep and lambs stood at the far end of the pasture, silently ignoring us.

The Lambys grew up to be healthy and happy ewes, mingling indistinguishably with the rest of the sheep. But every once in a while one will break ranks from the flock and bolt over to get an ear rub or to head-butt me in the knees. Then, as though she is suddenly embarrassed, she scurries back to the grazing flock, covering up a moment's indiscretion.

The Chicks Are in the Mail

It's spring, so each day our mailbox is stuffed with seed catalogs—all good reading. But it's the colorful hatchery catalog that gets our family's attention. Chic chickens such as red-combed Buff Orpingtons, black and white Barred Rocks, and feather-footed Black Cochins make up this *Who's Who* of poultry. The catalog pages are filled with chickens with exotic names, impressive pedigrees, and showy feather headdresses worthy of dancing girls at the Moulin Rouge. I'm in a quandary. So many chickens, so little space.

Ordering live chicks from a catalog? Murray McMurray, the world's largest rare breeds hatchery, has been selling chicks since 1917. Each spring people in search of layers and broilers order new chicks from mail order hatcheries. The chicks travel from hatchery to home compliments of the United States Postal Service.

Newborn chicks are amazingly resilient. They emerge from their eggs at the hatchery and are immediately packed into sturdy cardboard boxes with ample air holes, and mailed overnight delivery to chicken fanciers across the country. Amazingly, the chicks don't need to eat before they travel because they pack their own internal snack—the unabsorbed egg yolk they carry inside their bodies that nourishes them for 48 to 72 hours.

"Chick Day" is marked on our calendar. So it's no surprise when the local post office calls at the crack of dawn with the message, "Your chicks are here." And so I hop into the car and head to town. The postmaster meets me at the back door of the post office and hands me my order. I flip open the top and a crowd of downy multi-colored chicks stares up at me with alert black eyes. I smile, wondering what I must look like to them—

Gulliver to the Lilliputians. I gently close the lid and scurry with them to the car so the baby birds don't get chilled. I turn up the heater and listen to a chorus of cheeping on the drive home.

By the time I get home, Doug has already made a home for the new chicks. In an old farm building called a brooder house, the traditional place on a working farm where chicks were raised, he's set up a heat lamp, waterer, and tray of chick feed—all sitting on a thick layer of newspaper. Home sweet home.

Our first task is to introduce the chicks to water. Since they are rushed from shell to box to postal delivery truck in a matter of minutes after hatching, they haven't experienced their first drink, so it's our job to introduce them to water. I carefully pick up a chick (they are even lighter than they look) and dip her beak into the water. Startled by the new sensation, she smacks her beak a couple of times and swallows.

After all the chicks have been "dipped" and their thirsts have been quenched, they huddle together, wing to wing under the heat lamp. The combination of warmth, water, and feed seems to plump them out after a few hours. Within a day they are eating ravenously, flapping their tiny wings with flightless urgency, and hopping around every inch of the brooder house floor. Our little chicks mature quickly, growing taller and gawkier until, like the ugly duckling in the story, they transform into sleek, beautiful birds.

The transition from egg to egg layer takes about six months. Young hens start laying slowly, producing one egg every three or four days. Often these eggs are humorously small—a little bigger than a quarter. Eventually, the girls increase their egg size and frequency to two eggs every three days. Some overachievers lay an egg a day.

May Flowers

The calendar says it's spring, and so do the red-winged blackbirds busily clambering in the ditches searching for nesting materials. In Iowa, winter can linger through April—like an unpleasant houseguest who's packed up the car to leave but stands in the driveway to chat inanely for a while longer. But May, lovely May, is safely out of bounds for winter. And nearly overnight, in Oz-like fashion, our yard sheds winter's austerity. And the divas of the spring garden, lilac and peony, burst into bloom.

Showy, large-headed, and sublimely fragrant, the lilacs and peonies grow in this yard thanks *not* to Doug's or my good planning and labor, but to the gardeners who lived in this foursquare farmhouse a long time ago.

When our house was built in 1903, it must have been an imposing figure on the landscape. Rising two stories from the earth, the white frame house with its sloping green roof cast a large boxy shadow on the treeless prairie around it. And so the owners set to planting parallel rows of silver maples for a windbreak on the north side of the house. On the sunny south side, they created circular beds of colorful and fragrant shrubs and perennials.

With the faith in the future that gardening teaches, these believers (and those who lived in the house after them) planted small lilac saplings along fencerows and gnarled peony roots beside the driveway. They dropped to their knees and sifted through the soil with the expectation of spring bouquets, summer bounties, fall wonders. But did they envision that someone like me might be waxing poetic about the fruits (or more appropriately, the flowers) of their labors in the following century?

If there are ghosts on an old farmstead, surely one of the places they exist is in the landscape. The rambling roses, the flowering quinces, the phlox, as well as the peonies and lilacs, all tell a story of our home's former inhabitants who surrounded themselves with their idea of order and beauty. It's lovely to think that these gardeners linger on in the unfurling of a rose bud or in the fragrance of phlox. Ah, if only these spirits could weed the garden...

"What variety are these peonies?" people ask me when they see them abloom in the side yard. But I've found no name for them. Perhaps they didn't sell well decades ago, so these peonies can't be found in any gardening catalog of today. Just-barely pink with a frilly head of petals, this peony has bloomed reliably for years and is one of my favorites, but has somehow fallen out of favor with the rest of the world.

It's the same story for the phlox in our garden. Tall, fragrant, and unencumbered with the mildew problems that can plague modern phlox cultivars, our lavender phloxes also have mystery names, mystery origins. Yet their namelessness doesn't bother them, and they return year after year without any care or concern from us. These, and many other old-fashioned flowers, make up the hundreds of varieties that once graced the dooryard gardens of turn-of-the-century homes but are no longer in commercial cultivation.

Perennial flowers are sometimes the very last remnants of long gone farmsteads—the bright whispers in the landscape that tell the story of a once bustling piece of land. A land that supported people and animals who joined together to work it. A land that was well tended and decorated with the flowers that still stubbornly bloom each year. If you look hard as you drive through the countryside, you may see vestiges of gardens—the phlox spires that bloom midsummer amid the wooden wreckage of an old house, the towering canes of flower-studded hollyhocks, the roses scrambling across the ground in full bloom.

There is such a place near our house. The vacant farmstead was purchased by the highway department to allow for a much welcomed road widening project. The house and outbuildings were razed, but curiously, at the far end of the property sits an upturned chicken house. In late spring, right on schedule, a circle of orange-red Oriental poppies sends up their fragile-looking crepe-paper blooms through the weeds and tall grass that stand between the highway's edge and the sideways lying chicken house. The startling color and the persistent blooms always catch me off guard— and make me smile. What determination in plant form!

So, as I head into a new gardening season, I keep in mind that our garden is a shared experience with the past and future. That the daylily I plant today is part of a larger garden plan that is not my own. The trumpet-shaped, yellow-orange daylily blooms will carry on a tradition of setting down roots and naming the place that they bloom: Home.

The Color of Calm

Our old farmhouse is a continuous home improvement project. Just as we finish one thing, another part of the house falls silently into ruin. This Sisyphean loop recurred recently when our contractor, who was asked to replace the bathtub surround, notified us that the bathroom floor and walls were completely rotted. Inexplicably, he explained, our bathroom was hovering midair inside our house.

And so, par for the course, a small repair mushroomed into a full-fledged rehab. With the walls replaced, the floor retiled, updated plumbing, and a new tub and stool (well, why not?), all that was left to do was to repaint the walls. That was my job. And I was thinking of doing something flashy.

Perhaps this impulse to paint the bathroom a bright color was a knee-jerk reaction to the knee-jerk reaction I'd had twenty years ago when I moved into this house. The color scheme at that time was best described as "circus-y." Pepto-Bismol pink woodwork was surrounded by seizure-inducing wallpaper patterns. So room by room, my husband and sisters, and I scraped wallpaper. And as each layer reluctantly gave up its gluey grasp on my walls, I became more enamored with the absence of color. I sighed with deep relief each time I exposed the quiet white plaster walls that lay deep beneath the raucous wallpaper.

We never re-wallpapered. And we painted the plaster in only the lightest of colors. But after living with the calm and security that white walls bring, some mad and dangerous yearning for color surfaced. And as I stood in the paint aisle, staring down at the paint chips fanned out in front of me like a winning hand of poker, I felt giddy and reckless. And I heard myself say to the guy who mixes colors, in a voice I didn't recognize, "Let's go with this orange."

When I started painting, I had envisioned a warm color that would envelope me in comfort and cheer every time I walked into the room. Instead, as I slathered on color, the walls seemed to reverberate as though I were trapped in some horrible TV dream/nightmare sequence. The hue didn't conjure warmth or serenity. This color was like molten lava just before it spilled over the volcano lip and traveled in a river of fire down the side of the mountain in hungry search of unsuspecting villagers.

If colors could talk, this one—the one throbbing from my bathroom walls and ceiling—would be a blood-curdling scream.

Even my teenaged son Graham, usually oblivious to any home décor changes, stopped in the bathroom doorway, and pulled the earphones from his ears. "Wow, that's orange," he said, in awe.

Then he stepped through the door, smiling, and said, "It's like being inside a jack-o-lantern." I sighed. The slimy interior of a hollowed-out squash was not the ambience I was hoping for.

But what could I do? I had a gallon of it staring up at me from the floor like a glowing evil eye. So I continued to dip the roller into the tray and cover the walls with one, two, three coats of orange paint—the clothing color of choice for hunters and highway workers.

When I was done I couldn't decide whether I might grow to like it— after completing some sort of 12-step program—or whether I should place a basket of sunglasses inside the bathroom door so visitors could protect their retinas.

I was thinking the sunglasses would be the best idea because they would also hide my red and puffy eyes, teary at spending so much time searching out the perfect paint color, taping off woodwork, windows, mirrors, lights, and air ducts, and finding the right music-to-paint-by.

It was only several hours of my life that I'd never get back. There was no reason to feel bitter.

Bitter orange. That's what this paint color should have been named, not some namby-pamby name like "Spring Dawn" or "Glowy Embers." I had the distinct feeling, standing there looking at the walls, that someone at the paint factory had designed this color in response to a low performance evaluation. And in the moments before he was fired for complete incompetence (or color-blindness), he put it into production.

I was surveying the finished bathroom when Archer, our busybody Jack Russell terrier, ran up behind me. He'd been dying to get into the bathroom while I was painting, insistently poking his nose under the door. Although he now had the chance to run in, he stood warily at the threshold. They say that dogs are color-blind, but I had my doubts, since the first thing he did when he saw the walls was lower his head and cower slightly. This reaction was coming from a small dog who would joyously roll in manure when given the chance. Not a positive endorsement.

Take a deep breath, I told myself. Breathe in through your nose and out through your mouth—a quiet, cleansing breath. Okay, I admit I might have been a drama queen over all this. It's not like painting a room is an irreversible act. In a few hours, with several gallons of paint, I could restore the walls to the insane-asylum white that they had been for years.

But I didn't. And after several months of slinking by the bathroom door, my eyes averted, I can finally say that I am used to the color. And I like it. Really.

A Kitten Caper

"I think a kitten is stuck somewhere in the barn," Graham told me as I was sitting in my home office at work on a copy deadline.

"I'm sure it will be fine," I said, not really interested in stopping work to take a trek to the barn. "Kittens are very adaptable," I added reassuringly.

"All I heard was this sad mewing," said Graham softly.

It's a hard-hearted person who can ignore the plaintive mews of a kitten, much less the plaintive looks of a son.

"Okay, let's go take a look."

One thing about living and working in the same place every day is that I have a fairly good sense of what is normal farm activity. No matter how chaotic this life may seem to someone else, there is a status quo.

For example, if the sheep are rapidly zigzagging en masse across the pasture in the middle of the day when they should be snoozing in the shade, this is odd. And what it most likely means is that one of the dogs has decided to chase them for sport. Or when Riley, one of our donkeys, stood alone by the hay feeder seemingly staring out at the evening's sunset, I knew something was amiss. Donkeys just aren't awed by their natural surroundings, and even the most beautiful sunsets go by unnoticed. When I noticed that he was still in the same spot an hour later, I walked out to see what was up. He had stepped inside the hay feeder and was stuck, fixed westward.

Mewing sounds from an invisible kitten meant that human intervention was called for. Graham and I headed out to the barn.

In summer, our barn is eerily empty—the horses, sheep, and donkeys prefer to be out in the pasture sampling the new grass arrivals. In the quiet darkness, it was easy to hear the faint scratching and meowing sounds when we walked in. But it was hard to tell where they were coming from. After wandering around a bit, stopping, listening, narrowing down the area, we decided the kitten was somewhere in the tack room. We lifted saddles, peered under saddle blankets, and checked feed buckets, but no kitten was to be found.

The mewing continued. We stood still and listened harder. Graham placed his head against the wall and his eyes widened. Shades of Edgar Allen Poe—the kitten was inside the wall.

But how? We'd just built the tack room in a corner of the barn, covering the studs with paneling so we could hang up our saddles and other horse paraphernalia. I knew there were no holes for a kitten to crawl into because the room was entirely sealed in an attempt to make it mouse-proof. Then we looked up.

The barn loft. It's where the kittens had been born. And six weeks later, they were mobile and curious. Apparently one hapless kitten had somehow stepped into the narrow space where the loft floor connects to the overhanging roof, and tumbled down to the ground floor of the barn— and was now trapped behind the wall.

"I'll get a sledge hammer," Graham offered, a little too enthusiastically.

"Let's wait on that," I said, hoping to come up with a kinder-and-gentler Plan B.

And so we spent several hours attempting to rescue the kitten with food, well reasoned pleas, and a long rope. I'm an eternal optimist. But as I lie on my stomach dangling a horse's lead rope down a dark hole, whispering, "Just grab the rope, kitty," even I had to admit that we'd been beaten.

"Shall I get the sledgehammer?" Graham asked hopefully.

It seemed that force was our only option. So, a sledgehammer was eagerly procured from the basement and "Operation Kitty Extraction" had begun.

With the prospect of impending demolition, Tristan, joined us. We each placed an ear against the tack room wall and listened. The muffled mewing led us to the corner of the tack room, leaving two walls as possibilities. The first hole was going to be dicey. No one wanted to hurt the kitten we were saving, so Graham aimed high above where we thought the sound was coming from. And with a lot less effort than it took to put up the paneling, he made a hole in it.

The hole was big, gaping, and empty—the kitten's cries told us we were just a little off to the left. The barn studs made it impossible to reach sideways, so another hole was made. And another. A little too gleefully for me, my sons took turns bashing holes in the wall to set free the kitten. The fifth hole produced a kitten. Tristan reached down into the wall up to his elbow and pulled out a pansy-faced, gray tiger kitten who immediately burst into an appreciative purr. One missed deadline and a destroyed tack room later, we had a rescued kitten.

Farm life is not always filled with happy endings. But on this day we had one. And all we needed was a little teamwork—and a sledgehammer.

Horse Sense

When I was eight years old I informed my parents that I needed a horse. No doubt I delivered this verdict with my hands on my hips. Amused, they asked where I would keep this horse. We lived in a 1960s ranch-style home in a new, treeless suburban subdivision called Fair Meadows. Needless to say, there was nary a fair meadow to be seen from any window in the house.

"Under the stairway," I replied. I'd measured the area beneath the stairs to the basement and I knew that a 13-hand horse could easily be stabled there. I was confident that I'd covered all the angles. In fact, I judged that at this point my biggest decision was what I was going to feed the horse: Whole oats and alfalfa hay? Cracked oats and grass hay?

"Where will you ride?" my mother asked. Fair Meadows offered neither bridle path nor green belt.

"I'll ride in the park," I said, imagining how I would use the jungle gym as a hitching post. I have to admit, I still hadn't worked out the details of getting the horse up and down the stairs from the basement. But I knew my horse would be well trained, and that a narrow flight of steep stairs wouldn't be a problem for him. I imagined myself ascending the basement stairs on horseback and bursting out of the back door, easily clearing the back stoop *National Velvet* style, and thundering down the hill in our backyard. My vision ended just before the chain link fence at the end of our property.

I continued to offer suggestions to my parents about how horse ownership could be successfully achieved; they didn't seem inclined to get on board with the dream. Then, when I was ten, my father hit upon what he must have deemed a stroke of parenting genius. He gave me fifty dollars. "Start saving for a horse," he said.

Well, that shut me up. I had seed money now and I was going to save for a horse. As it turns out, the financial opportunities for a ten-year-old girl in 1966 were, well, limited. By the time I had enough money for a horse, I needed it for a car. So I exchanged my dream of equine horsepower for the less flashy and more dubious horsepower of a 1972 Volkswagen bug (which performed its own version of bucking and breaking down).

But my dream of owning a horse never died. A mere 32 years later, on the day I was laid off from my favorite job—a galloping bronco ride at a dot.com—a respectable severance package enabled me to do the thing I never could as a child: buy my own horse. So I bought a handsome, 16-hand, 14-year-old, bay quarter horse gelding with four flashy white socks and a crooked blaze on his forehead that formed a white isthmus over one of his brown eyes. His name was Yukon.

To say I was smitten by this horse is an understatement. My husband was actually jealous. As I packed my riding gear into the car to head to the stable, Doug would yell out to me, "Are you going to see your boyfriend?" I visited the stables twice a week. Yukon's ears pricked up when I called his name. He nickered to me and nuzzled my pockets when I groomed him. Let's just say I'd had less attentive boyfriends.

Although I had taken a few months of riding lessons using the stable's schooling horses, I now started taking lessons on Yukon. As a new rider I was cautious, alert, and frequently paralyzed with fear. My instructor kept pushing me to go faster, harder, higher. But my speed, it seemed, suited Yukon, who didn't like breaking a sweat any more than I did. We were a good pair—a mature quarter horse who liked to eat more than he liked to run, and me—a mature woman who, I have to admit, likes to eat more than she likes to run, too.

There are a few fundamental truths about riding. The first, and most painful, is that if you ride, you fall. I've fallen off only a few times, and I can't entirely blame Yukon; in most cases, a more experienced rider would have stayed seated. Once Yukon reared up and I unceremoniously slid off his back and plopped into a muddy puddle seat first. (Lesson One: Hold On) Another time he spun suddenly at the sound of a plastic grocery sack rattling on a branch in the woods. I was flat on my face listening to his retreating hoofbeats through my velvet-covered helmet before I knew what had happened. I remember thinking, "Wow, you *can* hear hoofbeats on the ground—those Cowboy-and-Indian movies were right! (Lesson Two: Hold On Tighter) I'm thankful there haven't been many spills, and none that resulted in prolonged injuries—just bruised pride and a sore bum.

I've learned from horse ownership that with kindness, consistency, and carrots, it's possible to earn the trust of a thousand-pound animal who could easily crush me to death. I trust him, too. It's a powerful feeling to share trust with something so big. Finally, I've learned that the view from the back of a horse is different than the one from my own two feet. It's lighter, swifter, and sweeter.

Old Dog, Timeless Tricks

I had this epiphany as I was watched our Border collie, Rose, meander down the gravel road in front of me on our morning walk. Now in her fifteenth year, she was once the fastest thing on our farm. But time has slowed her gait.

When did that happen?

Rose was a "surprise" puppy. I was away for the weekend and Doug took Tristan and Graham for a Sunday afternoon outing to see a friend's litter of puppies. This "looking at puppies" business is a misnomer. No one in my family is a puppy shopper. We are puppy buyers. And so an afternoon's diversion resulted in our first Border collie, Rose.

Oh my, she was a darling. Square like a cinder block, her body was covered with a fluffy black and white coat that stood straight on end, making her look a bit punk, a bit crazy. To top off the ensemble she had one brown eye and one blue eye—called a china eye. That eye definitely got your attention when she looked at you.

And Rose had a way of looking at you as though she was momentarily considering speaking but was just pondering the right phrase. She never talked—she didn't have to. We knew what she wanted to do. Every living being on the farm knew. She wanted to herd.

She started with the cats. Farm cats don't suffer fools gladly (really what cat does?). They knew from past experience that puppies were not things to fear—they were to be toyed with, pushed around, insulted, roughed up for their lunch money. Yet in seconds Rose had 12 unflappable felines rounded up into a tight little ball on the patio. Their tails twitching in the air above them, the snarling clump of kitties looked up at me with irritation and bewilderment. "What's all this?" they seemed to ask.

Rose twirled a ballet of control around them, the front of her puppyish body low and menacing, her china eye staring them down with a stern, "Don't even think about it," look. We called Rose off or she would have collected farm animals in a circle for hours. When freed from their psychological imprisonment, the cats slunk off to their respective corners, muttering meow-oaths under their breaths with a distinct air of humiliation and resentment about them.

Even as a puppy, Rose established herself as top dog—and it wasn't by size or fierceness. It was by savvy, speed, and eye.

She seemed like a different species from our other dogs. Belle, a 100-pound Great Pyrenees, and Maggie and Duffy, mother and daughter Cairn terriers, looked at Rose with interest and wagging tails and welcomed her into the pack. But neither of these breeds, or the way they acted, prepared us for a Border collie.

Our giant white Belle was ubiquitous on the farm. Benignly stealthy, she seemed to be everywhere. Belle was there to see the kids onto the school bus. She was in the back pasture barking at coyotes. She was asleep on the front porch. In nearly every photo I took during her life on the farm she was either just walking in or out of the frame. After she died I kept seeing her figure like a friendly ghost—lumbering out of the lilacs, asleep in a sunny spot on the lawn, her undemonstrative but omnipotent presence still lingering.

Our terriers Maggie and Duffy were happy, alert, and in search of adventure—all the time. They twitched when they slept. Individually they were obedient—putting on this charade of loyal companion, looking you in the eye, a tail wagging. But together, they switched off their hearing—and their hearts—and they headed for the hills. Doug once found them attacking a badger. A badger is a cranky animal even on a good day, so these highly caffeinated dogs had him in high dudgeon. Too little to cause much harm, the Cairns had nevertheless worked Mr. Badger into such a rage that he was willing to take on Doug. (We later referred to this incident as when the Cairns sicced a badger on Doug.)

So I wasn't really prepared for the quickness of Rose. Or the engagement of Rose. She ran everywhere. (Why walk when running gets you there faster?) She would run up to me and sit down at my side, quivering, staring up at me—waiting for a job to do. She hung on my every word like I was just the most fascinating person in the world. But I rarely had enough "chores" to keep Rose satisfied—until, that is, she was old enough to go to sheep herding school.

Rose was simply a brilliant sheepherder. As her breed was created to do in the hilly Borders region of Scotland, Rose was eager and undaunted. She would run out to round up the ewes, her black and white body flashing a semaphore warning message. The sheep would catch one glimpse of her and panic, clump up, and run like one giant organism back into the barnyard. Rose followed close on their tails, urging them forward, steering them with precision in the direction she wanted.

Doug trained with her, using the old Scottish sheepherding commands of *Come bye* (bring the sheep back in a clockwise direction), *Way to me* (the opposite of *Come bye*), and *That'll do* (Stop!). But when I wanted to bring the sheep up from the back pasture, I didn't need archaic commands to jump-start Rose to the job. "Go get them," I'd say, and she nearly stood on her hind legs and saluted me—then ran off out of sight. Moments later, a thundering flock of sheep flew up the hill with Rose in controlled, but hot, pursuit. I'd do a quick head count, realize I was a few sheep short, and call, "Look back, Rose." And she'd slam on her brakes, spin around, and head back out to find the remaining evaders.

Watching Rose work the sheep was like watching a dolphin swimming or an eagle going in for the kill. She was splendid, all flash and fur, fueled by instinct. And loving every minute of it. You could tell she hated hearing the words, *That'll do*. Stopping was what Rose liked to do least when she was in the sheep pasture.

So sometimes now it's hard to recognize this slow-moving lass. Sure, she still likes to eye the cats, but she doesn't try to round them up. And we realized one day that she was stone deaf. But, she's alert, accommodating, and engaging—if you catch her china eye with a waving hand. When we have new lambs in the spring their larking presence stirs her up. She'll sit on the wrong side of the woven wire fence, body low, eyes locked on a lamb who hasn't yet learned the power of a dog. The lack of reaction doesn't seem to bother Rose. She is content to give the lamb a good stare down, then sashay back into her kennel for a long nap.

Sharing your life with a good dog is a wonderful thing. And because of the odd inequities of life spans, humans have the opportunity to live their lives with many dogs. And so I have taken that opportunity.

Every connection that you make in life—even with a dog—teaches you something. So here is the wisdom that Rose has imparted to me: That speed and superiority can come without swagger. That life is good if there's as much joy in work as in play. That true passion can ignite your life forever. And that you should never pass up the opportunity to sneak in a nap.

And that'll do.

Eating Close to Home

A friend of my teenaged son (and frequent mealtime visitor), Chance, watched with interest as I ran cold water into the colander of arugula I'd just picked from the garden. I scattered the freshly washed greens onto a large platter to make a salad for dinner.

"Hey, how come you guys grow your own food?" he asked, leaning his elbow on the counter. "Don't you have enough cash to buy it at the grocery store?"

Fifteen minutes later, after my stock lecture on the superior flavor of freshly picked greens, the health benefits of organic produce, and the physical and spiritual returns of gardening, I could see he was making a mental memo never to engage me in friendly conversation again.

In the past several years I've tried to develop a more personal relationship with the food I eat and serve to my family. By either planting it, raising it, collecting it, or by buying it from local suppliers, I know personally where at least half of what I eat comes from.

The garden where the arugula hailed from supplies us with a colorful array of leafy greens, herbs, onions, garlic, and heirloom tomatoes—the important ingredients in many of our favorite meals. We plant only what we like—no lima beans or okra for this family!—and just enough to fuel the evening meals that span the summer. Doug and I used to go overboard when planting, thinking, "You can't have too many tomatoes." But, in fact, you can have too many tomatoes. And take it from me, underused abundance is a guilty luxury.

We also raise chickens and lambs for market. In the spring, a box full of cheeping chicks arrives in the mail from a local hatchery. They grow from downy yellow chicklets to plump birds in about eight weeks. Last year we also raised our Thanksgiving and Christmas turkeys. In the late summer our ram lambs go to market. Organic and free range, the meat is sweet and tasty—and we know how they were raised, what they ate, and how they were treated.

We buy our beef from a friend who raises a rare breed (in the US) of Scottish cow called Belted Galloway. If cows were cookies this breed would be an Oreo. Its broad white belt (hence the name) is the creamy middle sandwiched between chocolate front and back legs. This farmer's operation is so small that it is barely a blip on the radar of the beef industry. But he raises his cows organically and with love. He tells me that his cows are so nice that he frequently hugs them.

Across the highway from our house grazes a small herd of ninety doe-eyed Jersey cows. They are the cream queens at our neighbor's family-owned dairy, Picket Fence Creamery. "The Girls" as I like to think of them, supply cream for my morning coffee, creamline milk (unhomogenized so the cream rises to the top), and ice cream so coveted in our household that it may necessitate a 12-step program.

Seasonally we go on collecting expeditions. In spring we hunt for elusive morel mushrooms in the woods. In summer we gather wild plums from the back pasture. And in fall the limbs of the apple trees in our yard are heavy with red and green fruit. And while the hens are happy and willing we collect green, brown, and white eggs.

Local farmers' markets in several surrounding towns keep us supplied with the produce we don't raise in our own garden—sweet corn, melons, and squash. We shop for locally produced chevre cheese, crusty loaves of artisan bread, and come home with bags of food as well as a sense of community that feeds our table as well as our spirits.

Are we food purists, culinary snobs, organic highbrows? Not at all. Open the cupboards in our kitchen and, amid the stone-ground pancake mix and organic honey, it's processed-food paradise. There are more images of Little Debbie peering out than there are photos of my kids on the refrigerator. I have teenaged boys, after all.

I wish I could tell you that my sons preferred fresh-picked peas to jelly beans, but I'd be fibbing (or writing my own revisionist history where I am one of those nutritionally superior moms). Although they have had ample opportunity to eat well, my kids nearly always choose food from the wrong column: Cheetos over cheese, puffy sugared cereals instead of oatmeal, and hot dogs—well, they'd eat hot dogs for every meal. Once when I was carping at Graham to eat better, he earnestly tried to convince me that the green Jell-O square on his plate was a vegetable.

But I'm an optimist. And patient. I like to think that the seeds of change my husband and I planted in their consciousness will sprout and bloom one day into a love of food that has a sense of place, history, and goodness. And that they'll want a connection to their food that exceeds opening the cellophane wrapping.

"The Girls" across the road, and their alluring array of ice cream flavors, may be just the marketing team that will win them over.

Hold Your Horses

Lush green grass. It's what our sheep, donkeys, and horses lust for in early spring. After a winter of dry alfalfa meals, the meadows around our farm look like a rolling endless smorgasbord to our animals.

But too much grass after a winter of dry feed can be dangerous. So we let our animals out on pasture slowly, much to their dismay. An hour of gorging, then back to the paddock where their digestive systems can slowly get used to the change in diet. Each day they get a little more of the green stuff until they can safely be "put out to pasture," a phrase that has negative connotations to everyone but grass eaters.

Too much grass too soon causes a condition called bloat in sheep. I remember reading a particularly vivid passage in the Thomas Hardy novel, *Far from the Madding Crowd,* where a flock of sheep gorge themselves on new grass and come down with bloat. Without going into the graphic details, bloat is bad—like indigestion that kills. In the Hardy novel the shepherd had to "lance" each sheep to release the stomach gas and save the flock—a rather unpleasant scenario that I would just as soon avoid.

But try to explain the dangers of overindulgence to my quarter horse Yukon, who stands with his head hanging over the gate, looking greedily into the pasture. He presses his broad chest against the bars, hoping for the gate to pop open. (Something tells me this tactic has worked for him in his past.) When I don't open the gate for him, he neighs loudly in protest. Then he stamps his foot to punctuate the unfairness of it all.

So one afternoon when I noticed the horses looking wistfully over the fence into our unmowed side yard, I thought, "What the heck." I'll just throw lead ropes on Yukon and our other two horses, Sam and Ben, and let them graze the lawn.

I felt pretty special leading my three beautiful horses around on little strings—like happy balloons bobbing up and down above the verdant lawn.

But there's a reason that you don't see people walking a bunch of horses around like big dogs. Once the boys realized that there was all that grass to be had, they got pushy and lost all respect for each other's personal space—and mine.

Before I knew it, Sam was standing on Yukon's lead rope and Ben's rope was underneath Yukon's right front leg. In less than two minutes of frenzied grazing, the horses were all wrapped up in an equine version of cat's cradle.

I was still thinking I could unknot them when Sam backed into me, pinning me against Yukon. "Gee, this isn't good," I thought. I pushed slowly against Yukon, who sidestepped enough for me to slide out of the tight spot. But to do that I had to let go of all of the lead ropes.

Sam, the drama queen of the farm, then reared up like the wild stallion he isn't—and ran off. Ben, not to be outdone, quickly galloped off after him. Like kites whose strings are unexpectedly severed, Sam and Ben pranced around the yard, kicking up their hind legs, giddy with their freedom.

But Yukon—steady, old, greedy Yukon—just kept his head down, inhaling the ground, lost in a happy grass-induced stupor. Ben and Sam enjoyed their game of keep-away for a few moments more, then started eating again.

Then we all stood calmly in the side yard, me following Yukon around with his lead rope in hand, and Sam and Ben coyly grazing about 20 feet away.

When I opened the gate of the paddock and walked Yukon back in, Sam and Ben were hot on his heels, not wanting to be left behind. Fiasco averted. At least this day.

Lesson learned? If I want to take a walk with animals, I'll take the dogs, not the horses. Insight gained? The phrase "hold your horses" is a lot easier said than done.

Backyard Archeology

In the early spring, when Tristan and Graham were small, we used to go out to the woods behind our house with a rake and a bucket and do a little rural archeology.

In the moist earth, amid the shallow roots of ancient silver maple trees, they found lots of treasure: tiny glass bottles with the metal lids still screwed on tight, white plate shards with blue flowers delicately encircling the edge. They even found an old pair of eyeglasses, sticking up out of the ground like the owner had dropped them a season ago.

The winter frost unearthed the oddest of things, pushed up out of the thawing and freezing ground. In the spring, the debris of the past farm inhabitants rose to the ground surface waiting to be discovered—to the pure delight of my busy sons.

"Look, it's a bell," screamed Tristan, running toward me waving a muddy hand, his cheeks blazing red with excitement. It was tongueless and now mute, but it was a bell—maybe from a bull or a cow. Graham found a fork, a spoon, and a collection of broken terra-cotta tiles. Every triangular rock was an arrowhead—even when it wasn't. They'd toss their finds into a bucket, then carry it to the hydrant to wash everything off.

They were systematic, excavating the wooded earth in sections. They would pull a rake behind them like a plow, and when the metal tines hit a piece of buried metal the "clang" would give away the hiding place. Then the boys would drop to their knees and start digging like badgers.

One year Graham's Christmas list had only one item: a metal detector. I think he was envisioning unearthing big treasure the following spring. And when he walked out into yard with his metal detector leading the way like a divining rod, he wasn't disappointed. It sang out over nearly every square inch of ground in our yard.

I could tell from his round eyes that he was expecting buried treasure—gold doubloons, jewel-studded crowns, rings and bracelets, perhaps a lamp with a genie. But I was expecting that he'd discover larger and more mundane things like an old engine or an entire tractor.

We had holes everywhere. And piles of booty. The buried treasure wasn't gold, silver, or diamonds, but farm machinery flotsam of the past fifty years—old discs, chain links, triangular harrow pieces. They found earth-taming equipment that had been discarded and swallowed up by the earth it once tilled—the earth having had the last word until my sons came along to release the prisoners.

The farmers of the early 20th century didn't have garbage collection services—nor would they have probably used them if they did. But they did have the earth and the means to move it. And being the efficient and self-sufficient folk that they were, they buried their garbage.

And years later the things that were discarded, but originally made to last—glass, metal, ceramic, stone—still lay silent in the ground waiting to be discovered and employed again.

Tristan and Graham had buckets of stuff they dug up, and they'd show anyone who came to the farm their treasure. And depending on the age and occupation of the visitor, the things they found began to acquire names and purposes.

The objects that my sons unearthed gave us all a window into our farm's previous work life. The rusted, dinner-plate-sized stars that we hung on the back of our garage were harrow disks that once broke the ground for planting. And the big wooden pulleys, frozen by so many years of inactivity, once did all the heavy lifting in the barn. With the enthusiasm and wonder of archeologists or gold miners, Tristan and Graham lifted chain links as thick as their wrists from the soft soil.

Several years ago a gusty windstorm felled most of the aging silver maples. When the wind stopped, the ground looked like a game of pick-up-sticks played by giants. We had a tree crew at the farm for a month. The windbreak planted on the north side of our house had lasted about sixty years—the life span of soft maples.

The absent trees opened up our view to the north and the ground to sunlight. We sowed the hillside with wildflower seeds and set a Celtic stone obelisk in the center in memory of the woods. A meadow of blooming flowers now covers the area where previously my sons mined the surface.

And beneath the flowering hillside lie generations of bottles and plate shards, old silverware, and farm tools, still buried there—intertwined with the roots of yarrow, poppies, and prairie grass—held fast in a secret embrace.

Finding the Elusive Fungi

Five thousand and forty-one. This is the number of morel mushrooms that my friend Khanh collected last May. She's a pro. So when she asked me to go morel hunting with her, I jumped at the chance. A chance to gather up these elusive and succulent fungi. And a chance to study at the foot of the master—or the mistress—of mushrooms.

"You can't tell anyone where this spot is," she said to me as she drove her Jeep down one gravel road, then another. My secrecy wouldn't be a problem because I'd lost track of where we were two miles ago.

When she pulled the car into an open field I saw the woods. The old-growth oaks and hickories hadn't yet sprouted leaves and stood like giants on the land with heavy open arms. She navigated her Jeep across the bumpy ground and stopped at the woods' edge, pulling into a thicket of small trees.

"Get your bag," she said seriously.

I'd been morel hunting before. I set out into the woods behind our house with Tristan and Graham when they were 10 and 8. Wiggly, active, alert, I thought these boys would be naturals for zigzagging across the forest floor in search of morels. Instead, they jabbed each other with sticks, stomped their booted feet into any open water they happened upon, and we came home muddy and morel-less.

But today I could feel that my luck was going to change as I followed Khanh into the woods. Dressed in knee-high Wellingtons, a long coat, and a hat, Khanh carried a walking stick for parting low-growing foliage in search of the stealthy morel. We had talked nonstop on the drive to the morel hunting spot, but now we were silent, walking through the woods, poking and prodding amid the spring woodland flowers and last autumn's leaf litter.

A walk in the woods in the spring is simply splendid. The moist ground releases the very scent of life: sweet, humus-y, full of possibility. Our target, the morel, was well camouflaged. Light brown, lumpy, and porous looking, some grow to be six to eight inches tall. Their cone-shaped cap looks like the everyday headwear of an elf or gnome.

Khanh walked on, her stick at her side. She would deftly kneel down, pluck something from the earth, and step on. By the time I caught up with her, I could see her bag was heavy.

"I left some for you. Did you get them?" she said, as she eyed my empty bag.

"Look down right now," she said, pointing at my feet.

I stopped and stared down, seeing no clue on the leaf-strewn ground. "Okay. What am I looking at?"

She gestured with her stick at an area two inches from my right boot. "Right there," Khanh said.

I looked harder. And what to my wondering eyes should appear, but a little morel standing like a soldier at attention. One step more and I would have flattened it.

Khanh smiled as I put the morel in my bag.

She strode on ahead, calling out "Look to your left, now. Veer more to your right."

How she could spot morels ten feet ahead of her was a mystery. She pointed out their clandestine locations with a flick of her stick and I eagerly plucked them up, feeling the weight of my bag increase.

When we got to the edge of a deep ravine we both stopped short.

"Wow, I bet there are a lot of mushrooms down there," I said. "Too bad we can't get to them."

No sooner had I finished my sentence than Khanh was scrambling down the slope. I gingerly followed, grasping tree branches and roots to steady me. Halfway down I lost my footing and rode the ravine all the way to the bottom on my bum.

Khanh rushed over to me. "Are the morels okay?"

The bottom of the ravine would have been a creek if it had been a wetter spring. Instead, the dry streambed gave us a path to follow, surrounded by vertical land on both sides that we scanned for mushrooms. Around a turn we stopped. Growing on the south slope was the largest cluster of morels I'd ever seen.

I'd always thought of morels as shy and solitary beings, but here they were en masse—a convention of them, a veritable morel metropolis. Big ones, squat ones, slender ones. A hillside morel village. I half expected Frodo Baggins to step out and bid us welcome.

But with one expert look Khanh could see that these morels were beyond their picking prime. Withering at the edges, these mushrooms would no longer be plump and tasty. So we stood there in awe for just a few moments more, then reluctantly wandered on.

When we were finished hunting, it was no surprise that Khanh's bag outweighed mine. But as generously as she shared her secret morel hunting spot with me, she dumped some of her morels into my bag to even up the score.

When I got home I didn't count my morels. I just admired each one as I lifted it from the bag and began the preparations for the mushroom feast I would make for dinner that night.

Gliding into Summer

In May the water at Lake Sundown is numbing cold. The morels have raised their spongy heads in the woods and the oaks are flushed with pale green new growth, but the lake water still holds the chill from the ice it was just six weeks ago.

Yet I'm willing to pit my kayaking skill against the possibility of overturning into the frigid drink. My kayak is a 12-foot-long, sapphire-blue vessel. In the early morning or just as the sun is ducking behind the trees on the ridge, this slender boat is the absolute best way to slip soundlessly across the glassy water to see what's happening around the lake's shoreline.

There's always plenty of action. A great blue heron stands like a statue in the shallow water of a wooded cove. When I get too close, he rises like a tired pterodactyl, squawking a raspy rebuke as he creaks into flight, taking several haphazard wing flaps before achieving airborne grace.

I kayak along the lake's edge, checking out the places that I've named, spots familiar only to me and to a few friends and family who have kayaked this way. Hanging Tree Point is a piece of land jutting out into the lake with a 25-foot-tall tree growing at the tip—hanging on like a horticultural high-wire act.

Bad Dock Cove is further on. Named for the quirky, bent little dock jutting into the water there, this inlet is also the home of Eagle Perch. The piece of land above the water features a huge graying, dead tree where we've frequently seen a bald eagle perched, surveying the water's surface for his next meal.

I continue along the shoreline saying out loud the places that have become my personal landscape, my lake vernacular: Rose Point, Buckeye Cove, Horseshoe Marsh. This topographical shorthand connects me to a larger naming tradition that started with the ancient Greeks and continues today in new suburban housing developments. It's the illusion that if we name a place, it's ours. Sort of a verbal flag staking.

My 14-year-old niece Oksana is more than willing to play along. She paddles quickly under Hanging Tree Point, ducking her head, then cruises across the middle of the lake like a Nordic princess, her long blonde hair shining in the sun. On the way back to the dock we cross over the humped back of Sea Monster Tree—a partially submerged, full-size water-logged oak. Single file, we paddle gingerly over the center of it, hoping not to scrape the bottoms of the kayaks and awaken the monster.

The best thing about a kayak is that it is whisper quiet. One morning Doug and I paddled into a secluded marshy area surrounded by waving willows. In a small half-moon bay, six deer grazed peacefully. Walking around them on the shoreline, eight Canada geese nibbled foliage. Standing to the right was a snowy egret. Just in front of him, a great blue heron was up to his knees in the water, hunting the shallows for fish. Nearby, a group of coots swam in leisurely circles. Off to the left, a painted turtle sunned on a log. It was like Mother Nature was putting on a play and this was dress rehearsal. We sat in our stealthy kayaks and watched this living diorama without attracting notice.

Spring rains make the lake water as muddy as it is cold. Secretive and dark, the water hides the lake bottom in even the shallowest spots. So when I'm kayaking about in the marshy spots of the lake, I often beach myself on a sandbar I can't see. Then I prop my paddle across my lap, sink both hands into the muddy lake bottom and scuttle backwards—like an upside-down hermit crab—off the sandbar back into deeper water.

Beneath the water's surface live fish—big, animated fish. More than once, I've been kayaking when a largemouth bass flipped out of the water less than a foot from my bow. Its pale body twisted in the air, then slapped back into the water.

Once when I was gliding through a shallow area I saw the pectoral fin— the size of the palm of my hand—of a large, lethargic carp. Three times the fin rose out of the water and waved back and forth. If I had been a character in a fairy tale, something enchanting would have happened next. But the fin disappeared into the water and I paddled on, having had the odd magical experience of seeing a fish wave hello at me.

I love the start of kayak season: The lake's welcoming slurp as the kayak slides in; the swift, exhilarating swish as the bow breaks the surface of the smooth water. Of course, I may change my mind about early-season kayaking the first time I flip over into the dark, frigid water. But until then I'll paddle slowly and carefully around the lake's cold edge, gliding soundlessly into Diorama Bay or Waving Fish Flats to see who's there to greet me.

summer

Summer Docking

The sweetest part of summer for me is spent in one of three places: on the water, in the water, or looking at the water. Growing up landlocked in the Midwest, I learned the meaning of relaxation and reflection from the ever-changing surface of a lake.

My grandparents had a lake house north of Chicago, on Loon Lake in Antioch, Illinois. Measuring just 166 square acres, Loon Lake was a puddle compared to Lake Michigan. But it was our puddle and it seemed huge.

Their house was called the Mackinaw House, although no one remembers why. It was a timeshare long before the term existed. The house was originally purchased by a group of guys—policemen, firemen, and blue-collars—who worked hard-and-dangerous jobs during the day and played poker every night in a South Chicago bar called Crowleys. They pooled their resources and bought a big boat of a house on Loon Lake. My grandfather, a regular at Crowleys, bought a share in 1948.

After a summer or two at the Mackinaw House, the owners began to pine for their seats at Crowleys, so they turned the garage into a bar. When our family visited, the men—my grandfather, father, and uncles—rarely left the dark building where they spent long afternoons playing cards, drinking brews, shooting pool, and dropping slugs into the jukebox.

My brother, sisters, cousins, and I spent most of our time on the dock, in the company of my mom, my aunts Margie and Patty, and the matriarch of the family, my grandmother Loral. We sat on lawn chairs or beach towels, talking, laughing, and telling the same stories over and over.

The most recounted dock tale was about my mom, who was famous for swimming from one side of the lake and back again one afternoon when she was 15. "I did it to impress a boy," she said. "I almost drowned," she'd deadpan, and everyone would laugh like loons. Which was the only loon sound I ever recall hearing. Loon Lake, oddly enough, had no loons.

I spent hours sitting on the dock, swinging my legs in the murky water and watching the bluegills swim up from the muddy bottom to nibble bubbles off my shins.

One summer my grandmother shrieked that she had dropped her much-admired diamond cocktail ring through the dock planks into the lake. A reward was offered, so my cousins, siblings, and I spent most of that summer under the dock, standing ankle deep in grasping mud, wearing facemasks, earnestly staring into the depths looking for a hopeful sparkle. At the end of the summer, my uncle Kenny recovered the ring under what I can only describe as suspicious circumstances, since he was neither wet nor muddy when he produced it from his pocket. In hindsight, the diamond ring/dock caper may have been the adults' way to reassert control of the dock. And since all the kids were under the dock, it was easy to oversee their safety in the water through the slits.

We didn't have a boat, which was just as well because, frankly, no one in the family seemed especially nautically inclined. Since it was a small lake, there weren't a lot of boats anyway, mostly compact motorboats with loud outboard motors that had enough zip to pull a single skier around the lake and back—a remarkably short trip that seemed to last forever if you fell off your skis and held on to the tow rope out of desperation. And there were fishing boats that crept restlessly around the shoreline looking for a good spot.

Summer was slow, liquid, and shimmering. Although the sun moved unhurriedly across the sky, it seemed that time itself stood still—accented only by the sounds of the day: the slurp of a wave breaking against the dock, laughter floating across the water on a breeze, the buzz of an unseen boat in the distance.

Loon Lake is a memory, and the Mackinaw House may no longer exist, but my love of lakes hasn't ebbed. So last year Doug and I bought a wild and wooded piece of property—it's a ravine really—that opens out to a sunny point on a small lake in southern Iowa. And before we did anything else, we put in a dock.

So now my summers have come full circle.

The dock is the perfect vantage point for watching the morning unfold. Deer step cautiously out of the woods to drink at the water's edge. A small flock of geese grazes grass along the opposite shoreline. A bald eagle sits on a dead tree limb coolly surveying the lake. From my lovely, low, and liquid horizon, I witness the scenes of the day: A cloud moves across the sun, and the water changes from blue to steel gray. The dark shadow of a descending eagle flies low across the surface. A splash shatters the stillness as talons pluck a bass from the water. The water shimmies and turns under the soft hand of the wind. Seated on my planked peninsula, I watch and wait for whatever happens next.

Something Afowl

Doug woke me up with the news that there was a strange bird in the yard. "It's big, white, and standing on top of the chicken house making a bizarre noise," he said. "I think it's a guinea fowl."

I wiped the sleep from my eyes and tried to recollect what exactly a guinea fowl looked like. Nothing came to mind.

I stepped outside to investigate and sure enough, there was a large white bird—about the size of a small turkey—atop the chicken house. Where he came from was anyone's guess. Guinea fowl are native to Africa, so this boy was a long way from home.

His head/body ratio (tiny head, big body) suggested that he would not fly into the house to do our taxes or split an atom. He stood there staring and blinking at us as though we were the odd ones. Then he opened his tiny yellow beak and let out an incongruously large sound. In fact, it was the silliest sound I'd ever heard. A really loud giggle.

The guinea fowl was still vocalizing in the farmyard when Doug left for work.

As I sat down at my computer to start my work for the day, the goofy guinea was still yodeling in the farmyard. Our terriers, Snap and Archer, were goggle-eyed at the back door, making nose prints on the glass, and drooling on the rug. I could hear the Border collies outside throwing themselves against their kennel doors. Everyone seemed darned eager to meet the guinea fowl.

When I stepped back outside, the terriers squeezed between my legs and made a mad dash to the guinea who was strutting around the farmyard. I was surprised to learn that the guinea fowl was quite the flyer. He sailed gracefully around the property then landed safely on top of the chicken house again. The little dogs went wild, jumping and twisting in the air. The guinea fowl let out a loud chortle and watched the dogs spin themselves into a frenzy.

I took Snap and Archer back into the house and they expressed their disappointment by howling like coyotes at the window.

DAY 2: The day broke with our rooster trying to out-crow the guinea. The rooster gave up dejectedly. The guinea had won Round 1 of the "Loudest Animal on the Farm" competition. A moment later, one of our donkeys brayed. A good contender, but the guinea started in and won Round 2. I sat up in bed and pondered, ironically, how all my friends say that living in the country is so peaceful and quiet. Just then, the rooster, donkey, and guinea fowl began an inter-species a cappella performance. Disturbing. I folded my pillow over my head, but the weird sound wended its way to my ears through the eiderdown.

DAY 3: The guinea geared up at dawn again. Perhaps he was lonely. For a sleepy moment (without the clarity that a strong cup of coffee brings), I thought that maybe he needed a friend. Then I imagined the sound of stereo guineas. He would just have to tough it out alone as a bachelor-farmer guinea fowl.

DAY 4: Feeling rather limber, I attempted to catch the guinea with a net. Even though he had a tiny head, it seemed filled with mirth at my fruitless attempts to snag him.

DAY 5: I tried to drown out the guinea calls by cranking up the stereo in my office. The music shook the windows in the house and blotted out the guinea's sonic lacerations. But it didn't take long to find even the soothing sound of Bach painful at that decibel. I decided to go for a drive. As I drove away, I watched in my rearview mirror the guinea chortling on the top of the garage like some manic automaton weathervane.

DAY 6: The guinea woke us up hours before our alarm had a chance to go off. I got up and drove to the local convenience store and posted the following note on the bulletin board: "FOUND: White guinea fowl. Quite melodious. Please claim."

DAY 7: The guinea was calling at the crack of dawn again. I returned to the local convenience store with a red marker and added the words "REWARD OFFERED" to the found poster.

DAY 8: I was speaking to a client on my home-office phone when the caller interrupted and asked, "What's that weird noise?" That's when I realized that I had gotten so used to the guinea's noise that I didn't hear him anymore. The guinea was no longer pecking at my last nerve. My client, however, asked me to call back on a clear line.

DAY 9: I spent 20 minutes watching the guinea eat bugs in the garden. Fascinating. When he was not screaming at the top of his lungs, he was on patrol in the flowers and vegetables. His tiny, arrow-shaped head darted amid the leaves, snapping up the grasshoppers that had been plaguing my garden.

We never did learn where the guinea came from. And, although not much of a songbird, I decided that he could stay at the farm as long as he wanted. Now that he had a job to do.

Blowing in the Wind

A windmill. If there is an icon that better depicts rural America, I can't think of one. Country landscapes are dotted with them. Some are the only remnant of occupation, marking the spot where a house and farm once stood. Windmills, built to harness the wind, pumped water from the ground for livestock, and the power it produced was clean, efficient—and free! Windmills were also built to last, and so they have. Some still twirl aimlessly in the breeze above acres of crop or grazing land.

We had such a windmill on our farm. The structure was sound. The tail was still affixed at the top, but the propeller head was stashed safe in the barn. As long as we had owned the farm—25 years—the windmill had never done what windmills were built to do—catch and employ the wind.

Then I found out about the Windmill Wizard. His name is Jim Boll and he lives in rural Dallas Center, Iowa, about eight miles from our farm. When I called him and told him I wanted to restore our windmill, he was reluctant. He had a lot on his plate, he said. Rescuing windmills was time consuming, he explained. And they were everywhere—windmills in need of his help. I didn't push him; I just wanted to get on his list. But by the end of the phone conversation, he said, "I'll be right over." And he showed up in my driveway 11 minutes later. This should have been my first clue that Jim Boll was a little obsessed with windmills.

We exchanged our hellos and he hopped the gate and strode into the barnyard where the windmill was. Jim walked up to the windmill base, looked up, and without hesitation scampered up the narrow ladder to the top.

Nothing could have surprised me more. The windmill was, at a minimum, 75 years old. No one had scaled the structure in years (except a few young boys who I grounded the minute I saw them past the fifth rung). So who knew how stable it was?

It wasn't so much that Jim climbed to the top with such speed, it was that he was perched at the top, straddling a narrow bar, where the wooden platform had long ago rotted away, and was swinging the head of the windmill around in a circle, ducking as it nearly decapitated him on each revolution.

I knew I was afraid of heights, but I never knew I was afraid of heights while I was standing on the ground. "Please come down," I whispered. But Jim Boll kept twirling the big head of the windmill, making the 7-foot tail clatter around in a big circle in the sky. He was shouting things that I couldn't hear because the wind caught his words and tossed them away. Then just as fast as he ascended the tower, he zipped down the ladder and was standing on the ground next to me telling me what a great windmill I had.

When he saw the propeller blades in the barn, I thought he was going to do a cartwheel. "These are great—no rust, no bullet holes." No bullet holes? "These blades are in the best condition I've ever seen on a Woodmanse of this age," he told me.

My windmill had a brand name? That question led Jim Boll into a whole new discussion of windmill makes and models, history, brands, types, eras, vintages. Ours was an "oil bath" he explained, then went on to talk about how efficient this model was—something about ball bearings and an oil pan, and he lost me after about three minutes.

I went to his house to see his windmill collection. It wasn't hard to find his house. He has seven windmills erected on his property surrounding his farmhouse, and more than that in various stages of assembly. I keep thinking that one day, in a big wind, all those windmill propellers will spin like mad and yank his farmstead out of the ground, flying the whole property away like some sort of earthen Spruce Goose.

True to his word, Jim Boll fixed our windmill. He lowered it to the ground using a big truck and crane. Then he did an assessment of the gearbox, added new ball bearings and fresh oil, reattached the blades, and lifted the windmill and set it back into place.

And for the first time in more than a half century, the great windmill propeller turned on our farm. The windmill casts a bigheaded shadow on our house and barn as the sun sets in the west. Seeing the spinning shadow, hearing the soft whisper as the blades churn the wind, it's like something has been set right on our farm.

And it's all thanks to the Windmill Wizard, who is, no doubt, hard at work fixing another windmill—setting in motion what time has tried to stop.

I Love a Parade

With the strains of Harold Arlen's "I Love a Parade" playing brightly in the back of my head, I set off with my son for his first parade in the small Midwestern town where we live. Tristan was three at the time and in a total lather over the prospect of going to a parade. He was even wearing his "parade hat," a jaunty cap with an orange propeller twirling on the top.

It wasn't hard to spot the parade-starting point. A colorful clot of vehicles, people, and animals were milling about without apparent purpose. Riders on horseback were trying to calm the nerves of their mounts who were glancing white-eyed at the troupe of musket-wielding infantrymen from a Civil War reenactment club. There were pickup trucks, fire trucks, semitrailer trucks. Pony carts and golf carts. Giant hay wagons and kid-powered red wagons. The Pork Queen. The Parade Queen. Everyone in town who had wheels, a costume, or a sash was lining up.

We headed toward Main Street, which was already lined with eager viewers seated in lawn chairs. We'd brought a blanket to spread along the curb. Tristan clutched a large shopping bag in both hands so that he could collect candy thrown by parade participants. (It's like a sweeter, tamer version of Mardi Gras.) The conventional parade wisdom is this: The more you yell and wave, the more candy will be flung in your general direction. Tristan knew the drill and was ready.

We found an open spot next to the curb and spread out our blanket. Precisely at 10:00 a.m., the parade commenced with a cacophony of sirens. All the kids were startled into action by the first siren squeal and immediately bolted into the street to see what was coming. Lessons on parade etiquette quickly followed as respective parents reeled in their kids with firm instructions about staying at the curb.

Leading the parade was our town's new fire engine. It rumbled by us—cherry-red, shiny-silver, and ear-piercingly loud. The kids loved it. Firemen tossed candy out the windows as the kids scrambled below for the tumbling sweets. My son waved madly at the firemen and scored two jewel-toned suckers and three pieces of wrapped bubblegum. He clutched his bag tighter and looked up the street in expectation.

Next in line was a vintage lemon-yellow convertible with impressive fins. Waving from the back seat was a candidate for county supervisor. All of a sudden, out of nowhere, an object rocketed toward us. Before I could deflect it, it struck my son squarely in the forehead. Stunned, we both looked down as the object fell heavily into his lap. It was a Popsicle. The kind with two wooden sticks. We looked up to see where the flying frozen dessert had come from and we watched with wonder as the candidate in the convertible hurled more frozen missiles into the crowd. Who thought throwing Popsicles was a good idea? I made a mental note to cast my vote for this candidate's opponent.

My unflappable son picked up the Popsicle, unwrapped it, and stuck it into his mouth.

"Cherry" he said.

I grabbed another airborne Popsicle as it whizzed past my head and placed it, wrapper and all, on the cherry-red bump rising on my son's forehead. In a few minutes the swelling went down, so I peeled off the wrapper and sucked on the Popsicle while the high school marching band stomped by, playing a rousing Sousa number with accompanying flag and baton twirling.

Next, a herd of fringed Western-style riders on smart-looking paint horses trotted up. The horses' metal shoes made ringing sounds as they pranced past us on the pavement. The candy-less riders waved enthusiastically at the viewers. Toddlers were charmed by the horses, but the older kids, more interested in candy, slumped back onto the curb to wait for something more lucrative.

And the parade rolled by. The manic antics of Shriners on motor scooters dazzled us. A gray-cloud-spewing bevy of antique tractors chugged by us. A dog obedience club showed us how to heel, sit, and stay. With each lumbering John Deere combine, shrieking emergency rescue vehicle, and dawdling riding lawn mower, my son's candy bag grew heavier. By the time the last "float" arrived (a Model T Ford with the town's oldest man and woman shoehorned into the backseat), my son's bag weighed as much as a bowling ball.

As we walked down the tree-lined street, we viewed the remnants of the parade everywhere: Tootsie Rolls smashed flat onto the hot pavement, helium balloons caught in the limbs of trees, uncollected jawbreakers glistening in the grass like Easter eggs. Although Tristan was struggling with the weight of the bag, he looked like he'd won the lottery.

The parade was everything we'd hoped for. It was loud, long, and sugar-filled. We'd be back next year.

County Fair Time

As the corn grows high in the July sun (it's always much taller than "knee high on the 4th of July"), you notice something else sprouting up along the highway: signs announcing the dates of the local county fairs. Midsummer is fair time and on small and large farmsteads around the county, 4H kids are grooming livestock, testing recipes, and sewing buttons onto newly made clothes. Winners at the county level go on to compete at the big event of the summer—the Iowa State Fair.

Nothing delivers a bigger helping of pure fun on a hot summer day than a trip to a county fair. And there's a little something for everyone. By tradition, county fairs are agricultural competitions, so the stars of the fair are the animals, vegetables, and farm machinery—the biggest and best in each category. In the barns it's a veritable zoo of domestic animals: milk cows, beef cows, pigs, sheep, rabbits, chickens, and horses. The exhibition halls display platters laden with baked goods and garden produce. Award ribbons mark the winners of such competitions as the best cream pie, the sweetest strawberry jam, and the largest yellow squash.

A favorite event for our family is the sheep rodeo. It's a tamed-down version of a real rodeo. Instead of wild mustangs or muscle-rippling bulls, the steeds of this event are low-to-the-ground woolly sheep. In place of swaggering chaps-clad cowboys, the riders in a sheep rodeo are small children. The short distance from the back of a sheep to the ground makes this sport more comic than dangerous.

In exaggerated rodeo style, the announcer calls out the stats on the first rider and his mount: a shy, but scrappy kindergartner named Jason is going to ride a woolly mammoth of a sheep who goes by the name of "Snowstorm." Jason straightens his cowboy hat, then without hesitation jumps into the shoot and lands squarely on Snowstorm's back. The announcer works the crowd with his voice, raising the level of excitement in the stands. The door opens and the pair hurtle out into the ring. Snowstorm looks like a windup toy on caffeine as she stops and starts around the center of the ring, trying to rid herself of her rider.

"Jason's got a good grip," the announcer thunders. "but Snowstorm's gathering steam!"

The ewe darts forward then stops short, and Jason lurches sideways off his mountain of wool and lands seat first on the ground.

"The blizzard is over," shouts the announcer dramatically, and the crowd goes wild. The boy, looking a bit sheepish on the ground, stands up and dusts off his Wranglers and walks stiff-legged to the fence, a smile creeping onto his face. Meanwhile another youngster is saddling up another wild-eyed ewe and heading out for the (albeit brief) ride of his life.

The revving of big engines catches my attention and they pull us toward the noise of a tractor pull. A tractor pull is a strongman competition for agricultural machinery. Instead of lifting barbells, these massive tractors drag a sleigh of weights across the ground. Competing tractors can weigh more than 6,000 pounds, and like wrestlers, each tractor competes within its own weight class. And it starts! As the tractor gathers momentum, the rear wheels spew dirt and gravel into the air. Black smoke billows from the exhaust pipes. The sound is earsplitting. We watch several pulls, including the winner, a souped-up John Deere tractor. But our attention span is short with so much to see, so we're off to another event—my sons' favorite. It's the most extravagant destruction of property in a sanctioned situation—the demolition derby.

This event is a fight to the death. A group of cars spars gladiator-style to see who will emerge the victor. A flag drops and the arena jumps to life. Old cars madly careen and crash into each other. As a car is rendered immobile, it is disqualified and dragged to the side. The winner of the event is the last car able to roll in any direction, no matter how feebly. If your own car has ever stranded you on a highway, a demolition derby will be something to fantasize about as you call AAA.

After all this entertainment we've worked up an appetite, and we head to the food stands. Fair food is in a class of its own. Corn dogs, pork chops, cotton candy, deep-fried candy bars—you can get them all on a stick and they taste divine. If it's bad for you, it's here—deep-fat-fried with powdered sugar sprinkled on it. We all indulge in a corn dog and wash it down with a syrup-sweet lemonade. The county fair happens just once a year and it's the perfect place to get our yearly fix of well-groomed farm animals, monster-sized agricultural machinery, and a smorgasbord of good/bad food.

When the Cats Are Away...

My family and I love to travel. As often as we can, we pack up the rolling suitcases and head out of town on an adventure. From the time our kids were little, Doug and I dragged them to far-flung places to experience the flora, fauna, and flavors of different countries. Our accommodations have included small family-owned hotels in Holland, a 19th-century gas-lit shepherd's cottage in Scotland, a converted barn in Spain, and closet-sized hotel rooms with exciting new plumbing options in Paris. (After I explained the purpose of a bidet, Graham (who was five years old at the time) wanted to use it every 10 minutes. Who needs a water park when you can play in a bidet?)

But our hearts are pulled in two directions. When we travel, we leave behind our beloved pets—six dogs, 12 cats, three horses, a flock of sheep, five donkeys, a chicken house filled with laying hens, doves in an aviary in the garden, and two wise-looking tortoises. All in all, we have nearly 100 mouths, beaks, or muzzles to feed and water. Twice a day. So in order to satisfy our wanderlust while soothing our guilty consciences, we hire caretakers to watch over our farm while we are gone. To keep the home fires burning, so to speak. (Or to put them out.)

This is easier said than done. I exhausted the family-member-house-sitter option almost immediately. My sister Jen has a dog who chases cats and a boyfriend who is allergic to them. My other sister Susie's Golden Retriever is an incorrigible chicken killer. And my brother Bob lives on a different continent. (Come to think of it, could he have moved away just to avoid house-sitting for us?) One friend would love to stay, "if only there were an espresso shop within walking distance." Other friends confess childhood fears of horses, phobias about birds, and allergies to wool. ("I can't even wear sweaters," one friend whines.) It appears that staying at our house is not for the fainthearted.

Our favorite pet sitter also happens to be our contractor Randy, who has done so many remodeling projects at our house that the pets—from dogs to donkeys—consider him a member of the family. The Border collies leap with joy at his arrival. The cats mob him in the driveway like he was made out of tuna. And the horses prick up their ears and whinny at him. St. Francis of Assisi wouldn't receive such a warm welcome. But there came a day when Randy wasn't replumbing, rebuilding, or refinishing something on our 103-year-old farmstead, and we had to look for alternative house sitters.

We learned quickly that not all house sitters are as capable as Randy. One gentleman misplaced both of our Cairn terriers, who were picked up running joyously down the highway just two hours after we left on vacation. We called home a number of times to check in and the house sitter claimed that although he couldn't catch the terriers, he could see them in the yard and was feeding them every day. This struck us as odd, but terriers are an odd lot so we shrugged it off. We got home to find that the dogs had spent the week with the local veterinarian, where they landed after the dogcatcher picked them up. We're not quite sure what animals the house sitter was feeding every day, but the sack of empties in the basement indicated he was drinking enough to see more than terriers.

Another house sitter was outwitted by our sheep—an animal not widely known for its intelligence and cunning. On this trip, we'd met my brother Bob and his wife Carina at a rental house on a small island off the coast of Sweden. The house was spacious, spare, sunny, and stocked with every modern convenience—except a phone.

We awoke late one morning to a persistent knocking on the front door. I opened the door to greet a small, white-haired man. He smiled shyly and spoke very slowly.

"Your sheep are out in America," he said in a heavily accented voice.

"What?" I asked, having no idea what this sentence meant in any language.

"Your sheep are out in America," he said again.

By this time, my Swedish-speaking sister-in-law Carina, stepped in and had a long conversation with the man. She started laughing. Then the man started laughing. Apparently a funny thing was transpiring—in Swedish. The rest of us waited for a translation with stupid smiles on our faces.

Carina said, "He's saying that your house sitter called and left a message at the village store, and that your sheep have escaped from their pasture at home."

Sure enough, our industrious house sitter was able to track us down to a nearly unmapped island an ocean away, yet wasn't able to gather up a small flock of sheep in his own backyard. We checked the time and determined it was too late to call home. The loose-sheep-in-America problem would have to wait another day. It gave us time to ponder the issues of wandering livestock and a seven-hour time difference. At one point after dinner (perhaps after a bit too much Swedish lager), we stood on the beach calling across the water, "Go back home sheep!" At the time, it seemed like the best solution.

The following day when we called the house sitter, we learned that our sheep had escaped through a gate he'd accidentally left open. They ran down the road in search of greener pastures, but came back home on their own after a couple of hours. We sighed in relief that our sheep were now back in—in America.

This summer when we go away for vacation, we've scheduled a bathroom-remodeling project so our contractor Randy will be at our house to do chores. The dogs, cats, and horses will be thrilled. But the sheep, with their opportunistic and wandering ways, may be disappointed.

Water Garden Wonders

I'd been on a conference call for an hour when I noticed the birds massing outside my window. Red-winged blackbirds were lining the branches of the ash and apple trees next to the driveway. On the top of the pergola near our water garden they were lined up, wing to wing. Below them was a group of blackbirds swishing about in the shallow water of the pond. I had a brief flashback of the playground scene in the 1960s Hitchcock movie *The Birds*.

Then I heard someone on the conference call say my name, and I was startled back into the moment. I realized that I hadn't been listening to the call; I'd been watching the birds.

"I'm sorry," I said, embarrassed. "Can you repeat that question?"

I came back to the conversation about an editing project I was working on, but I continued to watch the birds with interest. They kept flocking in—all queuing up for a dip in our 10x14-foot water garden.

I shouldn't have been surprised. The water garden is a magnet for life in all seasons. In spring, the pond quenches the thirst of migrating birds. In summer, the water is incubator to millions of births—from insects to amphibians—as well as home to our lacy-finned koi. In autumn, butterflies sip water on flat stones. And in winter (thanks to a pump and floating de-icer), the water garden functions as spa and watering hole for the overwintering birds in our yard.

Just steps from my house I use the garden as an annex to my office. Although the cordless phone works there, I usually leave it indoors so the timeless sound of water flowing over rock isn't interrupted by the persistent sounds of 21st-century technology.

When I'm working there I'm in good company. The siren song of water is very seductive. Our dogs get wiggly with excitement over the water garden. On several occasions they have joyously jumped in, only to be fished out with stern words. The farm cats stare into the water as though it's a fascinating movie that they've watched a million times, but still love. They optimistically stare into the water wishing for a fish, while they sit at water's edge with paws poised. (I've never seen one land a catch.) Even Tristan and Graham and their teen-age friends occasionally respond to the irresistible call of the water and wander to its edges to watch the water show of the moment. I haven't yet met the boy who can pass up the opportunity to fling a rock into water.

Beneath the smooth surface of the water garden is "home sweet home" for wildlife of all kinds: koi, goldfish, tadpoles, water bugs, and countless squiggly organisms that Graham once showed me under a microscope. The banks of the water garden reveal another bustling ecosystem. Toads, spiders, snakes, bees and other insects lurk in low-growing foliage that surrounds the water. *Fear Factor* could do a film segment in our garden.

But there's really nothing to fear. In fact, the diverse crowd of critters indicates we're running a clean ship. We are organic gardeners, and our "live and let live" horticultural philosophy makes our garden a safe haven for creatures great and small. I'm not wary of the four-, six-, and eight-legged inhabitants—nor do I seem to intimidate them. The crawling masses don't give an upward glance when my shadow darkens their door. And I know why. In entomology class—the study of insects—I learned my true place in the universe. Bugs outnumber human beings 200,000 to 1. Even though I'm the largest thing in the garden, I'm just an insignificant voyeur.

And watch I do. On May afternoons such as this one, the water garden is alive with commuting aqua life. Koi, with their swirling, gauzy fins, swim languorously around the bottom of the pond nosing over small pebbles in search of food. Their luminous scales flash orange, white, and yellow as they slowly swagger through the water. Friendly as puppies, they rise to the surface, poking their wide snouts out of the water, looking for treats, which, of course, I give them.

At the water's edge, hundreds of ink-black tadpoles clamber excitedly. In a few weeks they will sprout small limbs, and a couple weeks after that they'll drag themselves out of the water and hop off into the garden without so much as a backward glance. From egg to comma-shaped tadpole to wise-looking toad—this metamorphosis takes place in just six to ten weeks. It's like watching evolution on fast-forward.

This never-ending swirl of life at my feet offers new perspective to my work deadlines. If some creatures can live a whole lifetime in a week, surely I can complete an assignment in as much time. So, inspired by the serenity of the koi, the optimism of the cats, the meandering search of the butterfly, and the industriousness of the garden spider, I return to my office with lessons from Nature's mentors, and I finish up my work for the day.

Off to Auction

"Hey look! Maybe there's a skeleton in there," Tristan said, pointing to a coffin-shaped box wedged under a long table. "Can I open it?"

We had just arrived at an auction and were walking through the hall looking at the wares before the bidding started. My then-grade-school-aged sons had little patience for slow-moving auctions, so I was pleased something had caught their interest.

"Sure, go ahead," I encouraged, more than confident that the box would be empty.

Tristan cracked open the lid, then jumped backwards, letting it slam shut with a bang. I thought the theatrics were for the benefit of his younger brother, Graham, who hadn't had a chance to peek inside.

"Is someone in there?" I asked laughing.

"Yep," he said. Graham and I exchanged a look, and then opened the lid of the box slowly. Well, whaddya know. A skeleton. I lowered the lid gingerly and brushed my hands hastily on my jeans.

Like many small town auctions, this one took place in the local lodge hall. Most towns of a certain size have at least one: Elk, Moose, Grange, Odd Fellows. But unlike most auctions, this one was selling off actual lodge furnishings. It was an International Organization of Odd Fellows (IOOF) auction that was liquidating the contents of their halls that had closed throughout the Midwest.

I knew nothing about the Odd Fellows—except that it seemed to me that their organization name might be more of a deterrent than an invitation. I thought that perhaps "Nice Fellows" or "Fun Fellows" might have attracted more members. And although I had a lot of questions about the Odd Fellows—who they were, what they did—I didn't get any answers that day. Their belongings, not their philosophy, were the main event of the day.

We were at the auction at the request of my sister Jen. The day before she'd called me for a favor.

"There's an auction in Guthrie Center tomorrow," she said. "The ad in the paper listed 8-foot-long mission-style benches. I need one for my dining room. I have a meeting in the morning, so can you go and scope it out for me? I'll meet you there as soon as I can."

And so I went to do my sister's bidding—literally. Wandering amid the cast-off oddities of waning Odd Fellows Lodges, I spotted the benches and knew that one would be perfect for Jen's dining room. As I inspected the stack piled to the ceiling, I sent the boys off to unearth more bodies. (We later discovered that the skeleton wasn't real…thank goodness.)

"Who are these Odd Fellows?" I asked more than once out loud to no one in particular. They had the most interesting array of stuff I'd ever seen collected in one place—costumes, velvet ceremonial robes, big coffins, small coffins (the aforementioned skeleton), Roman armor. Whoever the Odd Fellows were, they had quite the sense of style and drama.

When I researched the Odd Fellows later, I found that The Independent Order of Odd Fellows (IOOF) is one of the largest and oldest fraternal orders in the United States. Founded in England in the 18th century, the first American Odd Fellowship was founded in 1819 in Baltimore. Their symbols include three intertwined rings representing Friendship, Love, and Truth, and the "All-Seeing Eye," a single eye that stared back at me from many an item of Odd Fellows memorabilia. The coffins and skeletons, of such interest to my sons, symbolized one of their philanthropic missions: the Odd Fellows helped bury the dead for those who could not afford it. They also supported widows and educated orphans. In a time when governmental social service organizations didn't exist, the Odd Fellows stepped in.

The bidding began just as I saw Jen pushing her way through the crowd toward me. When the benches went on the block, Jen bagged one for a good price. Then we settled into metal folding chairs with a piece of apple pie and the satisfaction that we'd gotten what we came for—at a good price.

When the Roman armor came up for bid, Tristan and Graham were back at my side.

"We want that stuff," Tristan said. Graham nodded excitedly.

And so I bid for them, their eyes moving back and forth between me and the auctioneer, until they were proud owners of four sets of helmets, shields, and spears. The whole lot cost $20. They were ecstatic.

We all ended up closing down the auction—watching with fascination as one odd thing after another was sold. The Odd Fellows had a good day, all in all. And so did we.

We helped Jen load up her bench, then tossed the helmets and shields into the back of the car. The spears wouldn't fit so we rolled down the windows on the passenger side and I laid the poles against the side of the car. Both Tristan and Graham stuck their right arms out the window and held the spears tight against the car.

Like victorious warriors returning from battle, we drove home on 60 miles of two-lane highways—our spears lashed to the side of the car, the wind whipping wildly through the windows, our pieces of armor rattling in the back seats.

Planting a Legacy

The act of gardening is a leap of faith. Every time you dig a hole in the earth and nestle a plant into the welcoming soil you create a pact with the future. And if you're working in a garden that you made—or are picking up where another left off—you are also keeping an agreement with the past.

Case in point: My friend Maria's garden. Maria and her family moved to upstate New York some years ago. They bought a lovely house with an established garden. The English-style garden was an homage to the White Garden at Sissinghurst Castle in Kent, a garden created by English writer Vita Sackville-West and her husband Sir Harold Nicolson.

The large half circle garden edged the entire backyard. It was planted in wave after wave of white-blooming plants—delicate umbels of sweet cicely, frothy spires of 'Bridal Veil' astilbe, fragrant sweeps of 'David' phlox, white bleeding heart, gooseneck loosestrife, *Cimicifuga racemosa*, and the autumn-blooming 'Honorine Joubert' anemone.

Of course, Maria was thrilled. As a gardener, she knew what a gift she had received (or really, in her case, purchased). The former owner and garden creator, who referred to herself as the "Mother of the Garden", asked for visiting rights. Maria, being the sweetheart that she is, agreed.

Spring came, and Maria, a great gardener herself, added a few of her own touches. When "Mother" showed up one day to collect some "babies," she surveyed the grouping of birdhouses that Maria had added to the garden to raise the focal point. Mother approved.

"I always thought about doing that," Mother said. And Maria breathed a sigh of relief.

But the garden that Maria tends every summer is not wholly her own. "The neighbors still refer to my garden as hers," Maria laughs, referring to Mother. "I guess you don't really own something until you leave it…"

Although Maria had never had a white garden before, she has kept it true to its original intention. And I know why she did it. I would have done the same. Because I love tradition. I love the thread of design, plant continuity, color, and form that connects one era to another.

Of course, living in a home—or moving into one—with an already established garden seems like a blessing. And it is, really. Flowers blooming, shrubs softening the edges around the house, trees spreading deep pools of shade. Hardscaping—patios, walls, pergolas, gazebos, follies. A planned landscape!

Wow, it's nice to live in someone else's dream. A ready-made vision in which to sip your coffee.

Last summer I interviewed a gardener in Ireland, Ruth Isabel Ross, and her husband John, who had a stunning garden that rolled out like a carpet from the side door of their Edwardian house. The unique design was incorporated into the landscape, a shallow bowl of land that was planted from one end to the other, a design created by the previous homeowners. The original gardeners were two sisters, one of whom had threatened to haunt anyone who changed the garden. Now, that's some pressure!

Keeping someone else's garden… It could have a downside. You might feel obligated, obliged, restricted, responsible. You might resist pruning. You could hesitate before moving a plant—even when it has outgrown its space. You maintain the existing color scheme. And there's always the possibility of a disgruntled visitor from the afterlife…

So as I head into this gardening season, surveying the gardens that Doug and I have grown, now in their twenty-fifth year, I see plants that were here at the farm long before I was including one rather joyous old rose called Seven Sisters—we've tip rooted her along the entire length of a 60-foot fence. She blooms only once each summer, but for two weeks in June she's the star attraction of the garden. I think about the person who planted it, whoever she or he was, and how pleased they must have been at this very same time in June when the rose looks so grand.

And, in some small moments, I think about who next will garden this land after we have passed it on? Will it be one of our sons who, at this point, are much more interested in music than mulch?

I settle on the idea that my spirit will reside here in the woodland garden, hovering low and near my favorite spreading bed of puschkinia bulbs. Doug, no doubt, will haunt the water garden. (He's there nearly every night in the summer having conversations with the koi.) And perhaps there is already the cast of previous gardeners—lurking shyly amid a wild tangle of trumpet vine—who added their touch of flora to the farmstead every summer since the house was built in the early 1900s.

The next gardener at our farm will have quite the congregation of shadowy but encouraging admirers—all there to witness another season of bloom.

Fence Defense

"Good fences make good neighbors," says the famous line from Robert Frost's poem, "The Mending Wall." I know this line—everyone does. But I didn't fully understand its wisdom until I found a white Charolais bull grazing in our backyard.

A good fence would have made the following scenario unnecessary: me running toward the bull waving a small stick I'd picked up off the ground, yelling gibberish in an attempt to shoo this big boy back into the neighbor's field. We fixed the hole in the fence that had invited him in.

Fences mean a lot to me. They are the single most important peace-keeping force on our farm. The fragile balance between predator and prey hinges on the strength of our fences and gates.

The chicken house fence keeps the raccoons from running in and introducing themselves with disastrous results. Raccoons are so clever. They have little hands—no opposable thumbs yet, but I'm sure their genetics are mutating toward the creation of one for each foot. They can open doors, pop off lids, probably drive a stick-shift truck. A fence—it's not a barrier, just a suggestion to a raccoon. To keep our hens safe, we built a large enclosed mesh run outside their house to allow the girls to set foot safely outside. The raccoons can only watch—and wish for wire cutters.

One night a mink slinked through a slim crack in the chicken house door. A mink's calling card is to eat only the heads of the helpless hens they kill, so the morning egg collection was a pretty gruesome sight. It's ironic that mink collars and stoles ever became fashionable. After seeing what they do to a chicken, the last thing I'd want around my neck is a mink.

One morning last fall I saw an illustration of how our fences enforce the balance on our farm. Two large coyotes were sitting just outside our woven wire fence looking in at our flock of grazing sheep. Good fences make good neighbors, indeed. Especially when the neighbors are hungry.

An open gate is an invitation to disaster. Our sheep, donkeys, and horses keenly watch the gates. If one is left open or unlatched they make a break for it. I don't think they want to leave us—because they always come back. Perhaps it's the allure of the open road, the siren song of the horizon.

Once our three horses found their way to freedom by stepping over a fence that sagged from a fallen tree branch. When a highway patrol officer pulled into our driveway (never a good sight), I ran out to meet him as he was getting out of this car.

"Do you have horses, ma'am?" he asked.

"Horses? Yes! Why?" I stammered.

As soon as I spoke, a horse neighed loudly. The officer and I both looked over to see our three horses, heads hung over the opposite side of our fence, staring into the yard at us.

"Those horses seem to know you, ma'am," the officer said.

"Have they done anything wrong?" I asked. "Caused a car accident?" (A real worry.) "Robbed a bank?" (An attempt at levity.)

"No, ma'am," he answered evenly. "They were just loose."

Relieved, I walked over and opened the gate. The horses galloped into the barnyard, loutishly bumping into each other, their heads low, ears down. Their body language expressed a little guilt—and a little glee—at getting away with something. But they seemed relieved, too, to step back inside.

Last summer the garden next to the barnyard was in full bloom—it had never looked better. It must have looked pretty good to the horses, too. Our stocky Haflinger horses, Ben and Sam, leaned in for a closer view, straining to nibble the tops of the blooms below. Their chests pressed harder against the fence until the old iron fence posts snapped off at the ground. The fence unfurled like a giant welcome mat and into the garden stepped Ben and Sam for an all-you-can-eat smorgasbord of strawberries, roses, and perennials. They ate their fill then stepped back into the paddock where we found them flat on their sides, snoring. The hoofprints in the strawberries gave them away.

Robert Frost's poem cautions, "Before I built a wall I'd ask to know/ What I was walling in or walling out."

Oh, I know.

Airstream Dreams

Silver Bullet. Tin Torpedo. A used Airstream trailer was on my wish list, and Doug and I had been shopping the papers and Internet. It was going to be our "test home" on 160 acres of land we owned. A little house on the prairie, albeit aluminum. We planned to roll it around from place to place to discover the perfect cabin site. Pull up by the pond, reposition near the woods, sit atop the hill—the Airstream overnights would surely show us the best place to build.

Shopping online, we found several models we liked and that were within our price range. But they were all located in far-flung places like Yuma, Arizona, or Walla Walla, Washington. (Weren't these towns in Warner Brother's cartoons?) So we kept looking for the Airstream of our dreams, hoping to find one a little closer to home.

Then one day Doug struck gold (or aluminum, as it were). There was a 1971 Airstream Land Yacht on eBay—located right in our town. Upon closer inspection of the tiny photo, a lightbulb flashed over my head. I knew exactly where this Airstream lived—just one mile from our house.

I'd seen the Airstream before. (They're hard to miss.) It was parked at the end of a lane next to a small white house in the country. On a whim one day, I pulled into the driveway with the idea of asking if the owners would be interested in selling. I was met by a 100-pound Rottweiler who stood up on his hind legs and slapped his muddy paws onto my driver's side window. I slowly backed down the lane beneath the stern eyes of the big dog. And then I totally forgot about that Airstream until there it was—online and for sale.

So we began the auction two-step, tossing bids into cyberspace and refreshing the computer screen to see if we were winners. My personal online auction strategy is to convince myself that I don't care whether I get an item, then lie in the fetal position on the couch with a newspaper over my head while Doug bids. The bidding was neck-and-neck. But Doug—and his nerves of steel—landed the Airstream. Then we hopped into the car, and two minutes later we met the former owner of our new trailer. (She was so much nicer than her dog.)

The trailer was as shiny as a nickel. And although it was 35 years old, only a true aficionado could discern vintage from new, because the basic design of the Airstream trailer hasn't changed since it was first manufactured in 1931.

"How can you tell the difference between your Airstream and your propane tank?" asked my friend Leslie as I was describing our new little home. She had a point. The silver Airstream and silver LP tank did look like twin pods from outer space sitting in our yard.

Before I could respond, she answered her smart-aleck question with a smart-aleck answer. "Oh yeah, the propane tank doesn't have windows."

Since our trailer had some years on it—35 to be exact—it needed a little remodeling. The essentials were all in good shape, so I set about changing the 3 C's of comfort—carpet, cushions, and curtains.

Curtains first. My mother, sewing guru that she is, took one look at the faded beige curtains and came up with a redesign—less tucking and pleats—to show off the funky brown-and-blue retro fabric I'd chosen. The fabric had a repeating pattern of small capsule shapes (just like the Airstream!). My mom mentioned—more than once—that the cloth was dizzying to sew, but she zigzagged her way through the creation of seven curtain panels.

My sister Jen helped de-carpet the trailer. On the hottest day of summer (bad planning), we slashed, yanked, and successfully extracted the faded floor covering from the trailer. We kept having to dash outdoors gasping for breath because it was so hot inside. Then, I laid wall-to-wall carpet in a foot-pleasing navy blue shag. Fitted snappy blue couch cushions finished off the look and the Airstream Land Yacht was shipshape and ready for her maiden voyage.

We cast her out onto the highway, headed south to our property, then launched her onto a sea of golden prairie grass. And we slowly trolled the swells of our land for a suitable spot to drop anchor.

Traveling Time and Distance

If I may edit a line from Mark Twain, The coldest winter I ever spent was my summer in Scotland. (Twain, in his typical acerbic way, was actually referring to San Francisco.)

It was our summer vacation in the British Isles. And it was a wee bit nippy.

We'd rented a house in the Borders area of Scotland. The shepherd's cottage was equipped with all the modern conveniences of the previous century. It was a snug two-story house that hadn't been modernized for decades. While it had plumbing (always a prerequisite in our family), it didn't have electricity. The lights were lit with gas and the house was warmed by coal. Looking at the description on the Internet, I thought, "How charming. It'll be like time travel." So we signed up. Off to 19th-century Scotland we would go.

Just getting to the cottage was an adventure. Driving south from Glasgow, every turnoff took us to smaller roads—from freeway to highway to road to lane. After driving some distance on a one-car-wide lane (the road etiquette is to pull over and stop to let oncoming traffic pass), we found the driveway to the property. The long drive passed by the main house and barns and led us to a farm field gate. Per our host's instructions, we unlatched the gate and traveled over a rain-rutted path across a sheep pasture to another gate. We opened and closed it behind us, and rumbled up a steep hill on what looked like a hiking trail. We braked for grazing ewes and lambs who ignored us until our front bumper nudged close enough to ruffle their wool.

After fording a bridgeless creek, we saw at last a stone cottage on the hill above us. We pulled the car to a stop and I dug through my bag looking for the photo of the house I'd printed from the Internet. This was it! The kids scrambled out of the car and ran to the front gate. Three sheep followed them into the narrow walled garden to the front door. The door was unlocked and we let ourselves in. (We dissuaded the sheep from coming with us.)

It was colder inside the house than outside. While the kids explored the upper floor of the house and called dibs on bedrooms, the adults—my mother, Doug, and I—poked around the ground floor. There were fireplaces in both the living room and downstairs bedroom.

"I guess I'll make a fire," said Doug, dubiously looking into the bag of coal by the fireplace. "How do you light rocks on fire?" he muttered as he settled in front of the hearth with a box of matches. Meanwhile my mother, Diane, put a pot of water on to boil and stood warming her hands over the steaming pot. I could hear the kids unzipping their bags in search of more clothes to put on.

After we got settled in the house, we drove to the nearest town to do a little sightseeing and shopping. Graham spotted his first souvenir of the trip. Rural Scotland isn't packed with souvenir shops, and unless you like things plaid (tartans) or things cooked in a sheep's stomach (haggis), souvenirs are few and far between, especially for a young boy. But Graham found exactly what he was looking for.

"I want slippers," he said.

So Graham got a pair of shearling slippers. I bought a heavy cable-knit sweater and a bottle of Drambuie. (There's more than one way to warm up in Scotland.) Doug and Tristan were eyeing rain gear. And my mom picked out a scarf that she wrapped around her neck while still in the store.

We were sheep-clad in plaid and suited up for summer in Scotland.

When we got home our fire was out, and the house was as cold as stone again. We made another fire and headed outside to wander with wonder at the landscape. The gently folding green hills seemed to go on forever. From our house on the hill, the only building you could see in any direction was the ruins of a 13th century castle. The kaleidoscope sky would change from clear blue to hazy gray to nearly black and back again. The weather would be sunny and clear then pouring rain all within the same hour.

In the evenings we took turns rowing on the loch and tried our hand at fly-fishing. The sun set late—around 10 o'clock. And once it was dark, it was darker than anywhere I've ever been. Except for the stars, which burned brightly above us.

Our little house glowed in the night. Inside, coal fires burned in both hearths and the softly humming gaslights made warm circles of light. My sons adapted fairly quickly to the lack of electronic entertainment and played one board game after another—shouting and laughing like they did at home in front of their video games.

By the end of the week, Doug was a whiz at making a coal fire. The kids were expert lamplighters. The sheep had learned to gather at our kitchen window after mealtimes looking for leftovers. And my mother and I had killed the bottle of Drambuie.

When we left the cottage for home, our luggage was packed with woolens and our hearts were a little warmer. Our toes, however, were still cold.

Fair Game

Summertime is fair time. In our area it starts with county fairs—99 of them to be exact, one for each county in the state of Iowa—culminating in the mother of all fairs: The Iowa State Fair. This fair is known in myth and song, literally. There were several film versions of *State Fair*—a musical based originally on the Iowa State Fair, with memorable songs written by Richard Rodgers and Oscar Hammerstein.

More than one million people attend the state fair every year. To indicate how impressive this is: the population of the entire state of Iowa is just under three million. Each day, the state's largest newspaper, *The Des Moines Register*, reports the fair's previous day's attendance as if this number is somehow a measure of our shared success. And it is, really, because visitors from all over the world come to our fair.

I have to admit, I'm a fair junkie. I go several days during its 10-day run. What's the allure? Sure, there's the food: things on a stick—corndogs, pork chops, fried candy bars. It's hard to find a salad, that's for sure (partly because it would keep falling off a stick).

My first day at the fair I head straight for the Turkey Federation booth for a grilled turkey leg. There's nothing like walking through a large crowd of people wielding a meat truncheon. It's so King Henry the Eighth. But flash-fried or chocolate-dipped food is just part of the draw.

Then I make a beeline to my favorite place in the fairgrounds: the animal barns, specifically the Avenue of Breeds, the Noah's Ark of the fair. There you can find a specimen or two of a wide variety of farm animals. Black-faced sheep, white-faced sheep, sheep with four horns. There are doe-eyed milk cows and blocky beef cows. Built-for-speed quarter horses and hardworking draft horses. There are chickens that look like fancy feather dusters, ducks that look like bowling pins, and rabbits whose ears hang down like a basset hound's. And a lot of animals you'd rarely see on a farm until recently—nouveau farm animals such as llamas, catfish, elk, and ostriches.

The fair demonstrates our love of extremes. The heaviest pumpkin, the biggest boar, the largest bull. And, the small fries such as bantam chickens, miniature horses, and hip-high cows.

The biggest boar garners quite the crowd. He looks more Buick than boar. And although I live in the country, if I saw this animal in my yard I'm not so sure I'd be saying, "There's a giant pig in my yard," as I called 911. Last year's big boy tipped the scales at 1,203 pounds, and its size alone made it look like something else—a hippo, a rhino, or a whale.

Last year Doug and I bought our new ram from a Wisconsin Cheviot breeder who came to show at the state fair. As it happens, we bought our ram before he won a blue ribbon. Our prize-winning ram doesn't seem to have a big head about being a state fair winner. In fact, he's one of the nicest rams we've ever had, due, no doubt, to all the grooming and gusseying up for a state fair competition. He's so gentle we could walk him down our road on a lead like a big woolly dog. (We don't, by the way.)

A couple of years ago we were in Scotland for the Royal Highland Show, their countrywide agricultural fair. And, to our surprise, it was just a small slice of the big pie that is the Iowa State Fair. Of course the Scots had different sorts of fair fare—breeds of sheep, cattle, and horses that were developed in the rough Highlands, single-malt scotch and honey-based mead from local distilleries, and stonewall- and wattle-fence- building demonstrations. But around the fairgrounds outside of Edinburgh, there were the same unmistakable smells—the sweet scents of cooking food mingled with the pungent odor of farm animals.

A fair is a celebration of all things agricultural. It's a moment to admire the abundance of the harvest, to honor the gifts of domesticated animals (fleeces, milk, cheese, eggs), and to pay homage to our agrarian beginnings, no matter where we now call home.

In the Heart of the Country

Since I live in the country, it's curious to me that my most memorable vacations are those spent in rural areas somewhere else—like the summer I packed my bags and left my country home and farm in Iowa to vacation at a country home and farm in Ireland.

Hilton Park in County Monaghan could hardly be called just a country home—it's a country estate. The bedroom suite in which Doug and I stayed—well, you could have fit the whole lower level of our farmhouse inside it.

The view out our window was simply stunning. The verdant green land unfolded like a sumptuous fabric, rolling out to the horizon with undulating hills, a deep blue lake, old oak coppices, and lush green pastureland. The land surrounding the estate was dotted with blocky white sheep, whose heads never lifted from the ground as they munched and meandered their way across this dreamy 500-acre property. In fact, the grass was so fresh, so delicious, that I made a small wish that we would have salad with dinner that night.

County Monaghan is north of Dublin and borders Northern Ireland. It's a county that many Emerald Isle visitors miss in their treks to the wild and craggy coastline of the west coast or in their pilgrimage to touch the Blarney Stone.

But I found that this landscape—simultaneously familiar and exotic—suited me fine. This was horse country. And sheep country. The land of small farms and large country estates. It was an ever-changing patchwork of landscape options—from spongy peat bogs and old-growth forests to wide-open rolling pasturelands and the deep blue waters of Loch Erne.

As I wandered around the grounds of Hilton Park, I was struck with how amazingly, almost dizzyingly, colorful everything was. The boxwood hedges in the parterre garden were the deepest green, the rose color was more intense than I recalled roses ever being, and the sky overhead was a brilliant, startling blue. I thought, "Oh, how I wish I were Irish."

Our host for dinner at Hilton Park was Johnny Madden, the current owner of the house and eighth generation of his family to live on the estate. The first owner, Samuel Madden, built the original house on the grounds in 1734. Johnny and his wife, Lucy, live at Hilton Park year-round to care for the house, gardens, and grounds—and to accommodate guests.

Seated at a large table in the formal dining room, we were surrounded by portraits of past homeowners, their faces looking down on us as we ate. As a room like this dictated, dinner came in several courses. And as luck would have it, I got my salad—greens that were grown in the organic kitchen garden.

As we were packing up to leave Hilton Park, I took one last long look over the green pasture, the bright blue sky, and the house sitting squarely on the top of the hill with a sense of permanence and nobility. I glanced back at the calmly grazing sheep when, all of a sudden, a red streak caught my eye—like an errant brushstroke in this pastoral masterpiece. It was a fox, wending his way through the grazing sheep. Surprisingly, nary a ewe lifted her head as this cunning predator ran by.

"I saw a fox in with the sheep," I told Johnny as he stepped out the front door to bid us good-bye.

Johnny explained that this was the fox's mode of operation. In all seasons, Mr. Fox traversed the pasture, enabling the sheep to become familiar with him and his scent. This scarlet runner innocently skittered across the field so often that the sheep eventually took no notice of him.

And here, Johnny explained, was how the fox earned the name "sly." When the ewes were in lambing season, the fox could wander in—unnoticed—and take his pick of newborn lambs.

And so my parting conversation at the elegant and comfortable Hilton Park was about livestock. And I thought, "I just don't get that far from home, do I?"

But I have discovered on this trip, as I have on others, that the heart of the country keeps the same slow and timeless beat—of seasons, livestock, gardens—no matter what country you happen to find yourself in.

autumn

Mice Capades

One morning I was in the barn to feed the horses and—What ho! There at the bottom of my grain bucket was a small mouse. Apparently, some ground oats lured him in and the slippery sides made it impossible for him to scramble back out.

There he was, in his soft gray-brown coat, gazing up at me with his patent leather eyes. He looked like a Beatrix Potter character who might, at any moment, say something pithy (in an English accent, of course) such as "Top of the morning to you," or "My, my, what a muddle I've gotten myself into."

"How cute," I thought as I reached my gloved hand down to gently lift him out, ready to wish him a jolly good day and send him on his way.

As soon as my hand came close, he jumped on like he was boarding the train to London. He ran straight up my arm, past my elbow, paused a moment on my shoulder, and then crashed headlong into my cheek. I screamed, shrugged spasmodically, and shot him back into the grain bucket.

Suddenly, I felt different about him. He looked less like a character from *The Tale of Johnny Town-Mouse* and more like the seamy nephew of Willard. I straightened up and thought for a moment.

"Kitties!" I called, and the cavalcade of farm cats came running. I headed back to the house for a strong cup of coffee before finishing the chores.

It was October and the mice were bedding down for the winter. In the few chilly days of fall, the outbuildings on our farm were thick with them. Our greenhouse became a rodent high-rise. Filled with two tiers of potted plants and a cage of garden doves, it was heated and packed with food.

The doves dropped ample amounts of seed onto the floor and the mice gorged below them—no doubt, loutishly laughing and squeaking with their mouths full.

When I opened the door to the greenhouse, it was like a scene from an all-rodent review of the Keystone Kops. They scurried into pots, out of pots, into the dove cage, out of the dove cage, up the walls of the greenhouse, then down again. I wasn't taking any chances, and took to wearing a hat inside, recalling the mouse-up-my-arm episode. A crazed rodent tangled in my hair would result in years of intensive therapy.

The mice were many—and destructive. So we bought traps. We tried them all: the snappy kind that catches your fingers as often as mice; the sticky kind that lures mice in—a kind of cardboard Venus flytrap; and several other versions of some company's attempt at making a better mouse trap. We opted for the finger-snapping traps, and Doug set them twice a day.

He would come into the house after morning and evening trap patrol with a body count. (Frankly, he was a little too gleeful about the numbers.) But even with all the trapping, the mice continued to sack the greenhouse. They also took up residence in the barn's tack room and happily shredded lead ropes, ruined reins, and munched through the girth strap on my favorite saddle.

But it wasn't until they moved into the house that I felt personally affronted. With two Jack Russell terriers and three cats indoors, only the steeliest (or stupidest) of mice would set up housekeeping in our home. But one morning I pulled a cereal box from the cupboard, and standing behind it (like a game show prize behind door number 3) was a mouse. Instead of scurrying away in fear, he jumped right off the shelf as though he'd been up all night watching James Bond movies. He hit the floor running and disappeared beneath the stove.

Later I found that in addition to his cereal orgy, he'd also been dining in my spice drawer, and had eaten a whole packet of saffron threads that my sister Jen had brought back from her trip to Morocco. This was war.

With pets in the house, trapping was dicey. So we tucked traps into drawers and inside cupboards. Later, I would hear the sharp crack of a trap snapping shut, followed by a scream (and often a curse) as my teenaged sons found them the hard way when foraging for food.

I was making coffee one morning when our little boarder sashayed across the floor in front of me. I called the terriers who came tumbling into the kitchen and caught the scent immediately. The mouse ran under the refrigerator and the dogs shot after it, realizing too late that they weren't as small as a mouse, and smashed their faces, cartoon-style. They sat there all morning, wagging their tails in chagrin at missing the mouse, and full of anticipation at the prospect of meeting him again.

But he never showed his pointy little face again. Did the sight of two toothy terriers make him pack it up? Or did he have a run-in with one of our silent cats in a dark hallway one night? With a carnivore patrolling nearly every room, it would seem there were less dangerous digs in the world. So perhaps he simply whispered "Cheerio" in his crisp English accent and bid us adieu.

Driving Miss Daisy

"Hold the reins this way," my instructor said, as he repositioned my fingers.

I was seated in a lightweight carriage with bicycle wheels. In front of me was a 2000-pound black Percheron mare named Daisy who was pawing at the ground with her dinnerplate-size front hoof. I felt like I was sitting on a paper airplane equipped with rocket boosters.

I held the reins the way the instructor showed me, loosely woven between my fingers, with the remainder of the reins coiled in my lap like so much black licorice.

"Whatever happens, don't let go of the reins," he told me.

I nodded, thinking, "Not on your life."

It was Day 1 of a weekend horse-driving seminar that Doug and I had signed up for. At our farm, about 10 miles away, lived our three horses, two of which were trained to drive. We were here to learn how to drive them.

We'd come to this seminar having already mastered the wildly confusing art of tacking up a horse to drive. I draped and clipped the heavy leather and stainless steel pieces onto Daisy then threaded the reins from her head across her back to her rear. The action reminded me of threading a sewing machine. The tension had to be right or disaster ensued.

I took a couple of deep breaths and tried to feel serene. It was November and my hands were sweating in my gloves.

Daisy weighed a little less than my first car. A mere 75 years ago, Daisy was the SUV of her day. She would have been a veritable Hummer. Seated low and centered behind her massive flanks and twitching tail, I tried to channel this experience. But I just wasn't picking up on any past life experiences or collective unconscious. If my ancestors drove horses, none of them were stepping forward. It was just me, my sweaty hands, a cart with bicycle wheels, and a ton of horsepower in front of me. I was on my own.

I did momentarily ponder the unlikely details here. Horses are flight animals and I was sitting in a cart tied behind one. But on this cold November day, Daisy seemed less of a flight risk than just impatient to get moving. She shook her mane and the heavy silver hames rocked on her muscular shoulders, and every metal piece on her 200-pound harness tinkled like happy little bells. I guess I was ready to roll, too.

The instructor stood in the center of the arena and gave us instructions. We were to drive our horses around pylons set up in the center of the arena, guiding them in large figure eights. There were two horse-and-wagon combinations in front of me. When the lead horse took off, I expected Daisy to lurch forward in pursuit, but she stood still, waiting for me to give her the sign to go. Good girl. So I clicked my tongue, loosened the reins, and said "walk up." She stepped into action.

We were moving at a bracing 3 miles per hour, but the scenery was rushing by me at dizzying speed. I saw Doug standing on the sidelines waving.

"Speed up," called the instructor, and I loosened the reins a bit more and said "Giddy up." (We'd been warned not to slap the reins down on the rump of the horse—the way Hollywood movies make horses run.) Daisy sprang into a fast trot that I downshifted with a small tug on the reins.

We spent the day perfecting our driving skills on horses that were already perfect. Over lunch, Doug mentioned that our matched team of Haflinger horses at home knew how to drive, and that that's why we were there learning. Our instructor said, "How about if you bring them to tomorrow's workshop?"

Doug and I exchanged glances. It would be a great opportunity to learn to drive our horses as a team. We both agreed and both instantly regretted it. What if something went wrong? What if our horses freaked out? What if we looked stupid? Or what if someone got hurt? All distinct possibilities.

The next morning Sam and Ben loaded into the trailer like eager children. Off we went to the stable. When we walked them in, we realized how small they were compared to the Percherons. They looked like little Steiff toys—their long blonde manes carelessly crimped with curl and their heavy forelocks hiding their soft brown eyes.

The instructor, I believe, stifled a giggle when he saw them. Sam and Ben were draft ponies that measured nearly two feet shorter at the shoulder than the draft horses we'd been driving the day before. But they seemed eager, alert, and undaunted by the big boys who were shuffling and snorting in their stalls, so we followed their lead.

We tacked them up and walked them into the ring. When the instructor and his assistants moved Sam and Ben into position in front of a huge farm wagon, they stepped sideways with authority and stood stock-still while they were hooked up.

The instructor wanted to test drive them, and we all watched as he urged them into their first step. They leaned into their collars and the wagon rolled forward. In a moment, they were speeding around the arena with precision, spewing a tail of dust behind them. He got off the wagon and chuckled.

"Those boys have some power," he said.

Doug and I smiled. We felt like proud parents.

We took turns driving them around the arena. Driving a team of horses is like driving one large horse. The two horses are guided with just one set of reins. The right rein turns both of their heads to the right. A pull back on the reins signals them both to stop. The power of one horse times two. They pulled like a team and drove with accuracy.

As Doug and I headed home after the clinic, we knew we were a long way from harnessing up the boys for a drive into town. But we had taken the first steps to learn a forgotten skill that Sam and Ben already knew by heart.

Pressing Matters

When the fall air is as crisp as the apples on our trees, it's time for pressing apples into cider. Our cider-making tradition started not with the apples themselves, but with the purchase of an antique cider press.

"I bet this thing still works," Doug said as he twirled the wooden handle on the grinder of the old cider press. "In fact, I bet it cleans up just fine," he said, peering into the dusty maw of the hopper.

We were at a country auction and, by the looks and condition of the cider press, we'd be the only bidder.

I stared into the hopper hole to see an unappetizing mass of blackened gears.

"Ummm, cinder cider," I thought, but kept my thoughts to myself.

As I predicted, we got the cider press for a song. Then we tried to move it.

"Why is this thing so heavy?" I asked, incredulous that such a small object could weigh so much.

"Cast iron parts," Doug said admiringly.

When we loaded the press into the back of our station wagon, it sunk the body of the car low onto its frame over the wheels in a very unattractive, and possibly dangerous way.

"We'll drive slow," Doug said, as some sort of assurance.

We got the press home miraculously without grinding down the shock absorbers in our car, and awkwardly unloaded it into the garage with much huffing, puffing, and some colorful words.

"You don't have much upper body strength, do you?" Doug commented as we set down the heavy press. Wisely, I chose to ignore that question.

We'd bought the press just in time. This was the year of the apple, no doubt about it. The limbs in our orchard were practically groaning with the weight of all the fruit. Red and green hued apples hung like jewels, just waiting to be plucked.

Every year, this was my dilemma—what to do with all those apples? We'd all had our fill of apple crisp in the first two bakings. Sauce wasn't an option in our household anymore due to the veto power of my sons, who'd eaten too much of the squishy yellow stuff as toddlers. Most of the apples were eaten fresh off the trees or fed directly to our small flock of sheep. In fact, a few savvy sheep kept their hungry eyes trained on the yard, and whenever anyone meandered near the orchard, they started "bahhing" in a really naggy way. While the sheep cleaned up the wormy-and-windfall apple categories, we still had bushels of good apples. The cider press was the answer to our excess-apple problem.

Here's my little secret. After all the sarcasm and eye rolling over buying the cider press, I found out that pressing apples into cider was one of the most satisfying things I'd ever done. A cider press is an amazingly ingenious invention. A hopper in the top of the press allows you to dump apples in. A hand-powered grinder chunks the apples into bite-sized pieces that fall— core, skin, seeds, and all—into a mesh bag that sits inside a wooden bucket with slat sides. A chunk of wood fits into the bucket and you simply screw the wood down on top of the roughly ground apples and stand back as the golden rivulets of cider roll into a waiting pitcher on the ground.

"That's all there is to making cider?" we all wondered.

And it is.

We press apples the way Jackson Pollack painted—we toss in red-streaked Staymen Winesap apples with buckets full of tart Golden Delicious, often adding a flourish of Cortlands as an afterthought. One year, my sons heaved in heavy bunches of Concord grapes to make a dark sweet cider that was gone before the last turn of the crank.

Our cider days mark the end of the season, the end of the garden, and the end of the apples with a great sweetness that's good to the last drop.

The Hydrangea Heist

I admit, at the time I never felt a shred of guilt—and still don't. Several years ago, my sister Susie and I sneaked into a graveyard near her house at dawn to gather hydrangea blossoms. A cemetery. At dawn. It's creepy, isn't it?

That's how much I love hydrangeas.

Hydrangeas come in a variety of flower shapes. On the east and west coasts, the flashy big-leafed hydrangeas with cotton candy blooms stop traffic when in bloom. Growing hedge size, they produce giant mophead blossoms that change color based on the acidity or alkalinity of the soil in which they grow. (Acid soil makes blue hydrangeas and alkaline soil produces pink hydrangeas.) In the Midwest, where I live, these chameleons of the shrub world are not reliably hardy, but we have gorgeous white snowball and petal-packed paniculata forms that make up in beauty and flower form what they lack in showy colors.

It was these snowy blooms that caught my eye. The scene of the crime was a cemetery simply overloaded with huge, mature hydrangea bushes—big, sprawling shrubs that were laden from the ground to the tippy-top with extravagant Dairy-Queen-swirled blossoms. It was autumn and these heavy-headed white flowers were turning a wonderful russet at the tips—the same russet that is the accent color in my living room. Who can say what synapses spark in the criminal mind, but the amazing color coincidence was what, I believe, first led me to consider a horticultural heist.

As all good gardeners know, hydrangeas are best pruned right after the flowers fade in mid-summer, but these old plants hadn't been tended in years so a little nip and tuck would not hurt them a bit. A cemetery is an isolated place, a lonely place, a place without altruistic gardeners. Would these lovely, burdened beauties ever feel the caring clip of a good hard pruning? I thought not. And the more I thought about it, the more I felt it was indeed my civic, if not horticultural, obligation to trim up these long-suffering shrubs.

Initially, Susie was appalled when I told her my plan. Undaunted, I coolly dropped my Felco pruners into my purse. She gave me a dark look. She was going to have nothing to do with this caper; however, she agreed to case out the cemetery that afternoon with me.

I believe it was the sight of the glowing hydrangea blooms, each surrounded by a tiny nimbus of light—such as one sees in Pre-Raphaelite paintings—that changed her mind. That, and the fact that the large, russet-tipped blooms would look good in her living room as well. So Susie agreed to accompany me the following morning—with her own pair of pruners.

With all our justifications firmly in place (and our pruners in our purses) we hopped into the car at sunup. We took Susie's dog, Lily, as lookout. As we entered the cemetery, Susie killed the headlights and we rolled soundlessly to a stop. The sun was just peeking over the hillside and the hydrangea blooms glowed on the bushes with a light of their own.

In a matter of minutes, we'd each clipped a dozen or so stems and then run furtively back to her car with our floriferous bounty. The backseat of the car was crammed with hydrangeas. Yet, when we looked back at the shrubs to survey the damage, it was as if nary a bloom had been clipped—that's how many flowers these generous shrubs yielded. Somehow, reassured by the logic that if it doesn't look as though a crime was committed, then perhaps one wasn't, we drove away in satisfied silence.

Later at home, I placed the stems into a huge square planter with their big heads spilling over the sides. And in this same position they gracefully dried. Their russet tips perfectly matched my living room rugs. Three years later they still looked fresh, although they'd accumulated a fine layer of dust. (I haven't yet figured out an efficient way to dust dried flowers without producing a confetti of petals all over my floor.)

I did eventually go straight by planting several hydrangeas in my own yard. And it is with great pleasure that I watch them leaf out in the early spring, then produce chubby chartreuse flower heads that open in late summer to creamy white flowers kissed with a burnished bronze at the petal tips. And I'm also relieved that in order to get my hydrangea fix, I no longer have to skulk around graveyards at sunrise with my sister—armed with Felco pruners.

They Call it Puppy Love

It sounded like the wish of small child, yet it was coming from my husband, Doug.

"I want a puppy for my birthday," he said. I considered for a moment the pack of five dogs we already had and thought, "Sure, why not? What's another dog?"

"What kind of puppy?" I asked, suspecting that I already knew the answer. Three of our five dogs are aging Border collies. Rose, Floss, and Tweed were trained to herd our small flock of bossy sheep. In her youth, Rose was a black-and-white speed demon who could round up sheep, drive them into the barn, and make them do everything but tap dance. Her understudy, Floss, was fleet but a bit of a freelancer. And Tweed was all looks and no eye. He unceremoniously flunked out of sheepherding training with an exasperated trainer saying, "I've never seen a Border collie fall asleep in a field of sheep before." He's calm, he's smart, he's charming. But sheep aren't his thing.

So, it was just a matter of time before we needed to bring a new sheepdog into the fold.

"Do you have any prospects?" I said, knowing full well that there was a good chance that Doug had already gotten the puppy and had it stashed somewhere in the garage.

"Yes, I think I've got a good lead on one," he said. "We can pick her up on my birthday."

"Great. Where is she?" I asked, thinking that we were in for a weekend car drive.

"She's in Scotland," he answered with a straight face.

I smelled the sweet scent of conspiracy. Doug had cooked up this puppy caper with Sandra and David, a couple we'd met in Scotland two summers before. We stayed at their bed and breakfast, Achnacone Farm, near Appin, Argyll, on the west coast of Scotland, where they run a working sheep farm and Border collie training facility.

The wonders of the Internet. Doug was able to keep up with every litter of collies born at the farm through Achnacone Farm's website. And through email, he, Sandra, and David discussed bloodlines and herding idiosyncrasies. When Sandra bred Spot (a dog Doug admired on our first trip) to Slip (a fast-moving, easy-working sheepdog), Doug knew it was time for a new collie. Her name, he told me, was Nell, as he showed me a small photo of a tiny black-and-white puppy in an email Sandra had sent. And so began our odyssey back to the land of whisky, bagpipes, haggis—and Border collies.

We arrived at Achnacone Farm and it was much as we had left it a year-and-a-half ago. In fact, it is much as the entire 19th and 20th centuries have left it. The whitewashed, two-story 18th-century farmhouse sported inviting bright blue doors and small, deep set windows. In a wire kennel at the edge of the driveway, standing on her hind legs, was 10-week-old Nell, and her brother Ben (the Gaelic word for *mountain*). It was love at first sight all around.

It was a clear sunny day—a premium in Scotland—so we took Nell out of her kennel and headed across the sheep pasture for a walk. The air was a mélange of scents: wood smoke (or was it coal?) swirled with the slightly salted sea breeze, accented with the earthy fragrance of sodden peat. Sandra and her collie Nap were with us for a little herding work. At the far end of the pasture was a flock of yearling Scottish Blackface sheep. Small, hardy, and nearly wild, this is the national breed of Scotland and the hills of the Highlands are dotted with them.

Nell was a bit shy at first, but she warmed up fast and galloped around the field with glee—but always with a look over her shoulder at us for reassurance. Sandra called to Nap, *Away to me*, a command that instructs the dog to bring the sheep toward the shepherd from behind on the right. Nap moved the sheep up and right. The *Come bye*, command moved the sheep to the left. Right and left, left and right—Nap was leading the sheep around the field in a livestock version of the hokey pokey. Nell watched with interest, then as the sheep ran by us she dropped into a crouch and took off after them.

Sandra started laughing. "She's very fly," she said.

"Fly?" I questioned.

"Smart," she replied. "Look at that eye."

We watched Nell sprint after the sheep, then pull up short and come trotting back to us with a big smile on her face. Fly, indeed.

We stayed at Achnacone Farm for three days, walking Nell, hiking the 2,000 acres of bens and burns (hills and creeks) behind Sandra and David's house, eating well (Sandra's "mince and tatties" were a big hit), and admiring their thick-coated Scotch Highland ponies. Nell was coming home with us in a crate with her brother Ben, who was being picked up by a couple from Dallas the following day at our farm.

The day of our flight we got up early, packed up the puppies and our suitcases, and David and Sandra drove us to the airport—a three-hour tour that wove its way along the shores of Loch Lomond and through the towering peaks and untouched glens that were backdrops for the films *Braveheart* and *Rob Roy*.

The trip home was long, but traveling with a crate of puppies made us instant celebrities with everyone from passersby to the customs and airport staff. Puppies, it would seem, are the international passports to happiness. We gathered a giddy mob of high-pitched puppy lovers wherever we went.

Nell settled in right away with our other dogs and cats. She hasn't met our sheep yet. We'll introduce her when she's a bit older. For now, she's running around our house and romping with Tristan and Graham in the back yard. She's nearly house-trained, and comes when you call her name. And every day she shows us just how fly she is.

One Potato, Two Potato

The first time I planted potatoes I wasn't expecting much. An enthusiastic gardener, I knew the miracle that happens when tiny lettuce seeds sprout into foliage fountains. I had also felt the wonder of finding glistening strawberries, glowing like rubies, hidden among furry green leaves in the berry patch. But the dark mysterious ways of potatoes had never been part of my gardening repertoire.

Okay, I admit that I'm an instant-gratification gardener. When I first saw the shriveled, soil-stained seed potatoes—the parents of my future crop of potatoes—I was more than dubious. These tiny tubers looked lifeless, unpromising, and like a garden relationship that was destined for disappointment. But I planted them anyway, digging a 12-foot trench and setting in the seed potatoes about 15 inches apart. I covered them with soil, watered them in, and waited.

With any luck, my potato garden was going to be a veritable United Nations of tubers. I had planted exotic-sounding potatoes from faraway lands: red-skinned 'Desiree', the most popular potato in Europe; 'Russian Banana' fingerling potatoes; 'All Blue', with its distinctive purple skin and blue flesh, and the sweet-tasting 'Yukon Gold'. I planted them all (in separate groups) in a straight chorus line of spuds in front of our greenhouse, where they would have sufficient room to spread sideways if they needed it.

Much to my surprise, these sleepy tubers sprouted quickly, making great green mounds of finely cut foliage. Soon, starry white flowers with yellow centers appeared. My little potato hedge looked healthy and happy. And so it grew like this over the summer—getting bigger and greener. And beneath the soil's surface, in the subterranean world of worms, roots, and tubers, my potato seedlings grew slowly and with purpose. While my aboveground garden prospered and yielded bowls of arugula and lettuce and bushels of ripe, succulent tomatoes, my stealthy potatoes gained mass, silently multiplying and growing.

When it was time to dig them up at the end of the gardening season, I'd almost forgotten about them. The once robust potato plants had wilted and grown spindly. I went to the garden armed with a digging fork, garden gloves, a bushel basket—and high hopes.

What I discovered was this: Digging potatoes is like panning for gold. Thrust a garden fork into the ground and tilt it up, and you'll unearth a happy community of chubby and fleshy potatoes. The tiny seed potatoes I had planted in the spring had evolved into ambitious tubers that silently populated the earth around them with more of their kind. Nests of round, smooth skinned potatoes lay nestled in the earth, just waiting to be discovered. I knelt on the ground in front of the hole and lifted out large fleshy tubers with ease. My bushel basket grew heavy with potatoes as I moved down the line, unearthing the bounty.

I took my soil-covered potatoes in the wooden bushel basket to the garden hydrant and turned the water on them full force. The soil washed away quickly to expose a rainbow of colors: blue, red, yellow, and brown. The egg-shaped 'Yukon Gold' potatoes gleamed. The narrow fingerling potatoes (aptly named) looked gnarled yet appealing. The startling blue-skinned potatoes looked like lapis in the bright sunlight.

But my joy in digging potatoes was eclipsed by my first taste of them. Freshly dug, then boiled, homegrown potatoes taste nothing like their kin from the grocery store. We dropped the hastily washed potatoes into a boiling pot of water, cooked them until they were tender, drained them, and while they were still steaming, slathered them in butter, clipped fresh parsley over the top, and seasoned them with salt. Skins and all, we ate them. They tasted like the earth—sweet and delicious.

Of all the harvests at the end of the gardening season, potatoes are my favorite. As I lug the soil-covered potatoes to my cellar, I know that they won't last through the winter. And I'm already running through potato recipes in my head: mashed, boiled, fried—we'll be trying them all.

Planting Bulbs

Nothing looks less promising than a tulip, crocus, or narcissus bulb. Dried and flaky, they appear to be neglected onions that have been living furtive lives in the dark recesses of your cupboards. Yet, the fairy tale secret of bulbs is that deep within each one lives a flower waiting patiently to sprout and open. In fact, you can slice a hyacinth bulb in half and see the tiny intricate bloom, like a pale embryo, in the center of the bulb.

And with this beautiful metaphor and several bags of bulbs, I headed to my sons' school in fall where I was an occasional guest speaker on the subject of gardening.

It was my mission this day to explain bulbs and how they grow to a group of preschoolers. Graham was 4 years old at the time and I was the leader of his class field trip to the town square, where we would plant crocus in the raised beds. I came prepared with several bags of bulbs (more than 2,000 crocus) and as many trowels as I could wrangle from my garden shed.

At the preschool, the children were waiting for me, seated on the floor, arranged in a neat semicircle. When Graham saw me he waved shyly.

I set up my bulbs on a table in the center of the group, held one up and said, in my best teacher voice, "Does anyone know what this is?"

Hands shot up. Answers ranged from "something a dog eats," to "a smelly onion." Good answers one and all. I explained that a bulb has a flower that blooms in the spring tucked deep inside of it, like a little surprise package. The words "surprise package" had their attention. Then I cut open a hyacinth bulb to expose the hidden flower. There were "ahhs" of discovery and looks of earnest astonishment.

With the "classroom" part of the lesson behind us, we were ready to do some "hands-on field work." We donned our coats, hats, and gloves for the short walk to the town square. I set down the bags of bulbs and started to show the kids where we would plant them. I showed them photos of what the flowers would look like in the spring—tiny yellow and white chalices of bloom, some even bravely blooming in a light snowfall. I told the children that bulbs teach patience because you plant them in the fall, they sleep through the winter, and it isn't until the following spring that they show their stuff. The kids were looking up at me with rapt attention. This was going well, I thought, and briefly considering going back into teaching.

But in truth, I am more instigator than educator. And the more exuberantly I gushed on about how cool bulbs were, the twitchier the kids got. There must be a pivotal moment just before a group of individuals turns into a mob, but I didn't see it coming. One of the kids stepped forward, thrust his hand into a bag of bulbs and yelled, "Let's plant em!" Like a charge on the Alamo, multi-colored mittened hands started grabbing fistfulls of bulbs and tossing them willy-nilly into the open beds.

I looked for Graham for assistance, but he'd joined the other kids in this floral feeding frenzy. "Wait," I pleaded. "We need to make sure the bulbs aren't upside down." But my pleas went unheeded. The children were jabbing the gumdrop-sized bulbs into the soft soil so fast that, in a matter of minutes, all the crocus bags were empty. The bulb-planting melee was over. They'd planted two thousand bulbs in three minutes. Without even lifting a trowel. There was nothing left to do but say "Nice job kids," and head back to the preschool.

When I returned with the kids the school director was surprised.

"That was fast," she said, glancing down at her watch.

"We're very efficient," I said, sliding my unused trowels farther down into my garden tote.

That next spring, however, the beds were ablaze with crocus blooms. Somehow, although the bulbs had been tossed, shoved, and jammed into the ground rather than gently planted, these stalwart and forgiving flowers rose out of the town square planters as though they had been planted by true Dutchmen.

I walked through the square with Graham in the spring and pointed out our planting success. He was proud.

I think of this bulb success story often as I am planting narcissus, puschkinia, and scilla bulbs in autumn. I'm still struck with how miraculous bulbs are. How glorious they'll be as their blooms brighten the spring woods after a long winter. And how much I wish I had a crew of preschoolers at my disposal.

Autumn Hitchhiking

I'm a garden writer. Although this may sound like a pastoral, calm sort of career, the irony is that while I sit at my office computer dishing out sage horticultural advice, my own garden is under dramatic siege. As I am typing the words, "Fall is the time to be vigilant against weed seeds," these horticultural invaders in the surrounding fields are silently plotting to overrun my garden. And what's worse, they'll enlist the most unlikely of allies—my dogs.

Okay, it may seem like a long stretch (not to mention pathetic attempt) to blame my pets for making my garden weedy, but here's my story.

Crisp sunny autumn days are made for long walks in our back pasture. About midday, I often gather up our six dogs for a romp. The landscape this time of year is a mixture of burnished oranges, golds, and yellows. The dogs love to run through the weedy pasture, bounding ahead of me just far enough for adventure, circling back to make sure I'm still with them.

And as the dogs run joyously through the fields, they are unwitting participants in a plot so shrewd that military generals around the world would remove their hats in awe. Poised for invasion are millions of weed seeds, ready to become hitchhikers on my meandering pets.

This is how earthbound seeds travel. While the gossamer-winged milkweed or dandelion seeds can fly through the air with the greatest of ease to another location, the heavy, rotund, and sticky seeds of many weed species sit patiently on their grounded stems and wait for a ride.

These wily weed seeds must quiver with excitement when they spot Alba, our 100-pound Great Pyrenees, lumbering toward them. Like a canine combine, she gathers up seeds, burrs, and stickers in her thick white coat as she walks through the tall grass. Nestled behind her ears, ensconced in her leg feathers, seeds ride in soft, cushiony luxury. Alba is a mass transit line from the field to our garden—nonstop all the way.

Our fleet of fleet Border collies (Nell, Tweed, Floss, and Rose), like flashes of movement in the pasture, is able to slip in and out of fences like a pod of seals—then swim on through the bucking waves of grass. And on their travels, they pick up seeds from the wild grasses and cockleburs that grow in the fencerows.

Snap, our intrepid Jack Russell terrier, measures just eleven inches at the shoulder, yet she covers twice the ground—both horizontal and vertical—as the rest of the dogs. She leaps wildly through the tall grass, rising and disappearing like the periscope on a submarine. In her wiry coat she gathers round spiky sandburs, like a string of angry pearls, around her neck. They grab on and hold tight for the bumpy ride through streams and over hills.

The most obvious in their coats is the granddaddy of weed seeds—the burdock. The inspiration for the creation of Velcro, a burdock looks like an inert miniature porcupine. Oval and covered with tiny hooked spines, it needs all-terrain vehicles such as our roving band of dogs in order to migrate far and wide. The burdock seed is my nemesis. It's bristle-brush exterior seems to gather dog hair around it like the wearer of a shawl on a cold day. If I notice these burrs on the dogs after our walk, I can remove them with a stiff wire brush. If they elude me for a couple of hours, it's more than likely I'll need scissors to remove them.

On each romp through the pasture and fields, our dogs gather up all representative species of patient weed seeds and head home. These secret stowaways must be slapping each other on their backs at their good fortune. I marvel at the collection of weed seeds the dogs amass in just one outing. Brushed from their coats, these unlucky seeds will end up in the trash bin, yet I know that if I didn't take the time to weed my dogs, these seeds would happily plant themselves in our garden.

But it's only as Mother Nature intended. Nature strives for diversity. Even while I'm weeding our her handiwork next spring, I'll offer up a moment of silent respect for these plucky plants whose seeds outsmarted me and colonized with such determination where they fell.

Straight from the Horse's Mouth

I've read that people who spend a lot of time around horses are quieted by the relationship, but this isn't true of our farrier, Lyn. From the moment he steps out of his gleaming red pickup truck, to the minute he pulls back out of the driveway, this man is talking about something: West Nile virus, the land for sale down the road, the alfalfa harvest, the dry weather, the wet weather, the beautiful sunset last Tuesday. I turn off the radio in the stable and listen up.

The farrier comes to our farm every two months to clip our horses' hooves. Although he doesn't need my help when he works, I always arrange my schedule to be at the farm when he arrives. Along with his small cache of trimming tools and wide assortment of fashionable and functional horseshoes, he also brings information and news. *The New York Times* keeps me informed about world events, *The Des Moines Register* is my source for state news, and *The Northeast Dallas County Record* keeps me up to date on the happenings in the area towns and my kids' school district, but if I really want to know what's going on in the world directly around me, I ask the farrier.

A busy farrier like ours has a full appointment book. Every day he crisscrosses the countryside, driving from farm to farm to clip, trim, and shoe horses like mine. And as he travels, he picks up on the local buzz.

He delivers sensational front-page headlines about barn fires, wind damage from the last thunderstorm, and creeks jumping their banks. He offers weather forecasts and crop predictions. He's a veritable want ads section about what's for sale in the area: cropland, grazing land, horses of every breed, tack (both English and Western), hay, and stable bedding. He knows what businesses are starting up in the small towns that dot the countryside—and who's closing up shop. He mentions rumors of school district consolidations. And he keeps us informed of where to buy the best sweet corn of the summer (from the back of a pickup truck parked at the intersection of two county highways). Sometimes there's so much of interest, I need to take notes on the back of a feed sack.

The farrier is also our link to the outside world of horses. Our horses are homebodies and we don't often cross paths with other equines and their owners. So if we want to talk horses, we talk them with the farrier. Because he works so closely with them—and there's nothing that creates intimacy faster than standing beneath a 1,200-pound horse with his plate-sized hoof between your legs—he knows their moves, their reactions, and their nobility.

The trade of farrier hasn't changed much in the past 100 years. At the turn of the 20th century, farriers were a necessity of both farm and city life. They kept the horses of America up and running—the virtual pit crews for a fast-growing country racing toward the future. When the automobile made the horse obsolete as a method of travel and goods distribution, horses moved out to the country to become more pets than beasts of burden. But even in their relative retirement, they still need the services of a farrier.

And so, while the farrier gives the horses their well-needed pedicures, I quiz him about all things equine: what are his ideas about a horse-training theory I'd just read about, what's the best fly spray, does he think our horses are overweight or underweight, are their hoofs healthy, should I offer supplements to make their coats shinier? He has thoughtful and immediate answers to everything I ask. Then he smiles and shakes his head.

"If I'm reincarnated, I hope I come back as a horse owned by a woman," he says.

This is his way of telling me that he thinks I baby my three horses. I roll my eyes at this little criticism because he isn't telling me anything I don't already know. While he has been clipping, trimming, and filing down the hooves of my beautiful bay Yukon, I'm at Yukon's head, whispering into his ear that he is a good horse, a superior horse, the best horse in the world, in fact. Yukon watches me with calm eyes while I pet the white blaze that runs down his nose. I'm not embarrassed that I'm smitten with this horse. My farrier can't shame me.

But, of course, that's not what he's trying to do. Far from it. Most of his clients are horses owned by women. And the horses that he works with are all well fed, well groomed, and well loved.

While the farrier clicks through the local news, he expertly carves each hoof into a perfectly balanced semicircle. And as we talk in the barn, surrounded by calm and curious animals, I know that this is one of the ways I monitor the zeitgeist of the slow-moving world around me. Without so much as a phone line, a satellite feed, or an IP address, I learn about the tiny murmurings of my rural world in this oldest form of communication—a good conversation.

Keeping the Homes Fires Burning

"Do you think this fire is big enough to see from Mars?" Tristan quips, as he throws another branch onto the bonfire. Tristan is 16 years old and his conversations are a mix of sarcasm and understatement that, despite often skirting the fine line between humor and disrespect, usually crack me up. But I'm immune to smart alecky comments when I'm in the middle of a project I like, and there's little I like to do better than feed a bonfire. So, I keep tossing branches onto the fire, undaunted.

The fire has been burning for 10 hours. It started out as a building-sized brush pile in our pasture—the accumulated debris of the summer and autumn windstorms. We work around the edges of the fire tossing in branches and logs that had so far escaped the hungry flames in the center. The sun has set, the moon has risen, and the stars burn brightly above us while we work. The wood pops and hisses as the fire burns red, orange, and blue. The bonfire forms a circle of warmth around it that you can step in and out of like a room. As the fire leaps into the night, I'm warmed also by the idea that the Hubble Space Telescope might indeed see our bright little missive from Earth.

This night I'm dressed in my "burn outfit" which consists of jeans, Wellingtons, and my burn sweater—an olive green, rolled-neck sweater than has been so singed by flying cinders that, frankly, I'm surprised it hasn't totally unraveled. I suspect one last burn hole will reduce it to a pile of yarn at my feet. (When it does, I'll toss it into the great bonfire I've built.) I've also learned to wear a baseball cap at our family bonfires; once, as I leaned in to throw on a branch, the fire flared up and a section of my bangs disappeared with a whooshing sound. The unmistakable odor of burned hair told me of my mistake—which my hairdresser later fixed while slowly shaking her head.

Our family has always been firebugs. When my sons were small, on cool evenings in the fall we'd gather up sticks and limbs from around the yard and make a fire in the ring of fieldstones at the edge of the sheep pasture. With our backs against the darkness, we'd toast marshmallows or hot dogs on a stick. We were never alarmed at the sound of footsteps coming up behind us—it was just curious ewes stepping into the ring of firelight to see if there was the possibility of snacks. Their round eyes, with their odd rectangular pupils, would survey the scene. Then, not seeing anything they deemed edible, they'd step back into the darkness, punctuating their exit with long disappointed bleats.

Sometimes we'd sit around our campfire and talk with fake cowboy accents for as long as we could before laughing. Other times, we'd sing cowboy songs—or our version of them. Not knowing any authentic cowpoke tunes, we improvised with the only song I knew with the word "cowboy" in the lyrics: "Sweet Baby James" by James Taylor. My kids learned the words of this lullaby and would sing their hearts out at the top of their lungs: *"There is a young cowboy, he lives on the range, his horse and his cattle were his only companions. He works in the saddle and he sleeps in the canyons, waiting for summer, his pastures to change."*

I'm not sure where my fascination with fires comes from. I grew up in the suburbs in a house with an electric fireplace. A twirling red cellophane cylinder with a 40-watt lightbulb inside made silent, dancing "firelight" on our basement den wall. It could have been my elementary school stint as a Camp Fire Girl, though we weren't allowed to try our hand at fire starting at the basement meetings in our leader's home. Our family never camped; and although we pitched a tent in the back yard a couple of times, my dad was dead set against the idea of a fire that would burn a black hole in the lawn. So perhaps the love of fires in my adult life comes from the lack of them in my childhood.

If that theory holds true, my campfire-smoked sons will, no doubt, grow up to have an electric fireplace with a rotating cellophane cylinder of light.

Picking the Perfect Pumpkin

The weekend's goal? To find the quintessential pumpkin—a beautiful orange squash, sized somewhere between a basketball and Cinderella's coach.

So Doug, Tristan, Graham, and I set off to a pick-your-own pumpkin patch located about 30 miles from our house. Tristan was five at the time and he was wiggly with excitement over picking his own personal pumpkin. Graham was a toddler, so Doug and I spent a lot of time picking him up off the ground as we all walked across the pumpkin patch. Granted, a lumpy farm field crisscrossed with squash vines is not the best place to take someone who's learning to walk. But Graham was wearing a pair of corduroy overalls so we used the straps as a handle to lift him up into the air before he hit the ground.

We passed by some homely pumpkins, some looked more like flat tires or deflated balloons than perky potential jack-o'-lanterns. And there were big, unwieldy pumpkins the size of sleeping bear cubs too large to pick up or hoist into our car without the help of land-moving equipment. We patted them fondly on the back as we walked by.

Tristan galloped ahead of us. "Slow down," we called after him. "There are plenty of pumpkins." But he seemed eager to personally inspect each one. We followed, dragging Graham through the air by his overalls. Tristan zigzagged from pumpkin to pumpkin. His body language said, "too little" as he darted away from one. We watched him try to pick up another that was three times his body weight. He gave up and zipped on. He was wearing a blue coat with bright yellow sleeves and his little arms moving up and down looked like some sort of semaphore of excitement.

And then he was down.

We rushed across the field toward him, carrying Graham along like a marionette. When we reached Tristan, he was sitting squarely inside a rotted pumpkin.

"This one is too squishy," he said in the understatement of the day.

He looked too gross to even touch. He was coated in orange gelatinous goo. And every time he attempted to stand up, he slipped comically back into the shell of the pumpkin.

At last we got him on his feet and there he stood, sort of a slimed-up, vegetable version of Botticelli's *The Birth of Venus*.

Of course we did the bad-parent thing and laughed hysterically. Then we quickly did the good-parent thing and scooped Tristan up out of his pumpkin trap and headed for the car. He was as slippery as a fish, so it was hard to keep ahold of him. Luckily he wasn't upset. Being swallowed whole by a big pumpkin was exactly the type of adventure Tristan loved.

We got both kids back to the car quickly, afraid that Tristan would solidify into a pumpkin-encrusted piñata in the cool autumn air. Of course, since no one could have foreseen this type of mess occurring on such an innocent jaunt, we didn't have towels or wipes or anything that we could clean up Tristan with. So we just packed up our oozy offspring into the nice clean car. Getting a seat belt on him was a challenge.

On the way home we all discussed the wonders of rotting vegetables. And we were treated to the odors to match. It was a long ride.

We did buy a pumpkin, however. But not until the next day at the grocery store. Tristan picked it out from the safety of a shopping cart. And we later carved it into a beaming jack-o'-lantern. But I have to say that I always see a little smirk behind the smile now that I know what pumpkins are truly capable of.

Tornado Season

Since I live in the Midwest you might assume that I'm well versed in the angry and irrational ways of tornadoes. That every thunderstorm spawns funnel clouds that drop like Spider-Man out of the sky, tossing cows into trees and driving straw sticks into posts. And that as a flatlander, I share a meteorological bond with Dorothy, Aunty Em, and her little dog Toto, too.

But I'd never seen a funnel cloud until the Saturday I had my baptism by wind.

I live in an area where I can see weather rolling in for 20 miles in all directions. We've had straight-line winds yank our 50-foot-tall maple trees out of the ground like carrots. We've had skies overhead that changed colors like a celestial mood ring. But no tornadoes ever came calling.

I know that weather is a science and all, but tornadoes just don't make any sense. They stagger around the countryside like dangerous drunks, blowing up one house here, sparing another there.

Other violent weather, such as a hurricane, has an attention span. It knows how to focus and finish. But tornadoes seem to have Attention Deficit Disorder. They drop from the sky then pull back up again. Once on the ground, they indecisively change directions. Tornadoes do strange things like rip the roof off a house and leave a vase of fresh flowers sitting on the dining room table.

My tornado story (and now I have one) is this. Doug saw that there were hail warnings on television and stepped outside to check the sky. It was gray and lumpy but nothing unusual—until he saw the funnel cloud lurch out from behind the barn on the southwest corner of our property. He turned on his heel and ran into the house shouting, "Get to the basement."

But instead of heeding the hysterical directions from Doug, Tristan, Graham, and I ran right to the window (we were all on the second floor) to witness the tornado twirling toward the house. Oh my—no more explanation needed! We scrambled down two flights of stairs to the basement.

Huddled there, we watched the tornado lumber closer. (Only true nitwits seek shelter and then stand with their noses pressed against a window.) We saw a swirling wall of black soil and corn stalks come as far as our property line—about 30 feet from our house. Then the tornado traveled sideways along the fencerow, skirting the property's edge—giving the illusion that our rusted, 4-foot-tall woven-wire fence was actually keeping it out of our yard.

Seconds later it passed out of sight. So we all ran up the stairs into the driveway (nitwits, again!) in time to see the tornado cross the road and hit our neighbors' house a quarter of a mile away.

The tornado swaggered onward toward town, where it sliced through the south edge, ripping off roofs, blowing out windows, and moving one house like a chess pawn from one side of the street to the other. Then it tucked back up into the sky and disappeared. Amazingly, no one was hurt.

When we drove up the littered lane to see if our neighbors, John and Julie, were okay, we could see their two-story house was missing some exterior walls and most of the roof. Later Julie was amazed to find her dishes safe and stacked in the cupboards in what was left of the kitchen.

Their 150 sheep were crazy scared. They ran around smashed buildings, tripping over the dead power lines, trying to find safety. We helped to corral most of them, and began loading them into trailers for safer pastures. The next day, we found two frightened ewes trembling together in a weedy field corner near our house.

We surveyed our yard for damage. Not a thing was overturned, tilted, mussed up, or out of place—not the arbor, a terra-cotta pot, the glass chandelier hanging in the pergola, or a single shingle. How could it be that just yards from our safe haven there could be so much destruction? A house stripped of its walls and roof, a barn smashed, farm equipment strewn like toys across a field.

Later I imagined all the things that *didn't* happen to us. I hear the wrenching sounds of the roof being torn off the house, furniture being sucked out the windows, the sounds of breaking glass, popping power lines, exploding LP tanks.

And for months, with cinematic precision, I replayed in my mind all the things that did happen. Watching the black swirling wall of wind come closer, I was thinking how much I loved these people I was cowering in my basement with. Standing at the window, watching this angry beast scouring the ground beside our house, it seemed that my tall sons and pacing husband were some sort of force field against disaster. And I knew that if we all survived, we'd run outside, elbowing our way up the stairs into the emerging sunlight—shouting, pointing, and interrupting each other—giddy with the stories of danger and luck that we would tell forever.

Horse Play

In late autumn, after frost has turned our pasture grass golden yellow, our livestock continue to nibble away fruitlessly at the dormant blades. With less to graze, our horses eventually turn their attentions to mischief: they take up chewing on fences, pushing on the gates, and ripping off each other's halters.

I watched our blonde draft pony Sam pull the much taller quarter horse Yukon around by his halter one day. Yukon laid back his ears in anger, bobbed his head in frustration, and eventually broke loose. Then Sam would sneak up on him, grab his halter, and drag Yukon around some more. This went on for about an hour. I quit watching and went back to work.

When Sam got bored with torturing Yukon, he apparently decided to meddle with the water hydrant. And somehow he lifted the handle—a real feat considering he was doing it with his mouth. Since I didn't see him do this, I can only imagine what happened next: Sam watched the water fill the tank, then spill over the side, and walked off because his feet were getting wet. What I did discover later that afternoon was a lake in the paddock.

The next day I glanced out the window to see Sam and Ben, our other draft pony, galloping around the paddock, driving the sheep from one end of the pasture to the other.

The boys needed a hobby.

I checked the Internet for suggestions and in two clicks found a photo of a happy-looking horse with a big red ball in his mouth. A ball for horses? It was made from heavy-duty rubber with a handle, so any bored horse could pick it up and toss it gleefully around.

So this year Christmas came early to the farm—the day the UPS truck delivered a big box with a red rubber ball.

I walked toward the gate carrying the new toy. The horses watched me, their ears tilted forward in attention, their eyes locked on the ball. This was a very good sign. I stepped through the gate and I held it out. They all trotted toward me and leaned their heads in to smell it. The ball looked like a giant apple—their favorite treat. After nosing it for a few seconds, they stepped back in disappointment.

I tossed the ball into the air over their heads thinking a spontaneous game of equine soccer might break out. And in fact, they turned on their heels and galloped toward it. But once they reached it, they seemed not to recognize it. They surrounded it with suspicion, smelled it again, then reared up and reeled away. They spent the whole morning eyeing the ball warily and conspicuously avoiding it.

Maybe they just needed a little coaxing, I thought. I mean really, how would horses know how to play soccer if they'd never seen a ball before? I went back out to the paddock to show them how. My first kick caused a stampede of not only the horses, but the donkeys and sheep who were equally frightened by the flying red orb. The ball hit the ground, rolled a bit, and stopped.

I took a run at the ball and did my best Beckham. When my foot made contact, the ball made a loud thwacking noise and rose in a lovely arc across the paddock. Another stampede ensued.

"Doesn't this look like fun?" I asked the horses as I ran toward the ball and kicked it again. This time Yukon, Sam, and Ben just stood and stared at me. I think I may have heard snickering. All of a sudden I felt foolish, like a kid on the playground with no friends. I left the ball sitting in the middle of the paddock like a cheery beacon, symbolic of my misplaced enthusiasm, and went back into the house.

During the day all the animals ignored the red ball, giving it a wide berth as they walked around it.

But here's the thing: every morning the red ball is in a new place. Sometimes it's near the gate. Other mornings it's in the center of the paddock. It's not moving on its own. Is it Sam, Ben, and Yukon? Or have the donkeys struck up a game with the sheep? So far, I haven't a clue. But someone is definitely moving the ball around the barnyard at night. At last it seems the animals have a hobby: confusing me.

Latitudinal Longings

A honking v-formation of geese flies low and southward above me, framed in a square of bright blue sky. If I look long enough, their dark arrow seems to deliver a pointed message: *Go this way, go this way.*

It's a warm September day and all around me the air is filling with commuting birds. Geese, swallows, robins, blackbirds, hummingbirds—from the largest to the smallest of winged creatures—are packing up and heading out of town. Our yard is abuzz with bird busy-ness.

It's the start of migration. Songbirds, waterfowl, and birds of prey all over North America hit the skies, heading down an invisible superhighway that leads to warmer climes. Their latitudinal longings urge them to abandon the places they've called home and raised a family. Our robins are headed to Texas. The great blue heron that fishes our creek is Florida-bound. The overachieving barn swallows have set their sights on Argentina. The purple martins are winging to South America as well.

What tells them to go? The changing color of the leaves? The shortened hours of sunlight? The first frost? Even ornithologists aren't entirely sure how migrating birds know when it's time to pack it in and head south. Without a sound or signal obvious to humans, Mother Nature drops the starting flag on the great race southward to warmer weather.

The barn swallows are the first to leave. They've spent a productive summer swooping high and low throughout the yard and pasture, snapping up beakfuls of insects for their babies in the barn. Now all the swallows in the county, it seems, have massed together in dark queues lining the electric wires as far as the eye can see. The next morning they are gone—leaving their mud nests in the barn rafters like so many empty pockets.

From out of nowhere hummingbirds plummet into the garden with Napoleonic attitudes, type-A personalities, long beaks, and whirring wings. Like iridescent flashes of neon light, they zip from flower to flower, sipping nectar from the bell-shaped blooms of petunia, red salvia, and trumpet vine. They boss each other around the yard with sharp squeaks that sound more like electric current than birdsong. Then in the blink of an eye, they flit onward in search of the next garden and their next sugar fix.

Turkey vultures cast dark shadows on the ground as they ride the thermals above our house. Grackles and red-winged blackbirds, often traveling south together in mixed flocks, fly in like dark clouds. They swoop en masse like schools of fish, their dark forms undulating and changing shape—a living ebb and flow of birds—followed by the quiet hole of their absence.

As the leaves drop from the trees, the creative architecture of the birds' summer stay is revealed: the haphazard nests of great blue herons, the pendulous teardrops of orioles, basketlike robins' nests, and tightly woven finch nests, artfully constructed with the tail hair of our horses. Like the abandoned ruins of a lost culture, the empty nests tell a tale of architectural savvy, industry, and society.

Birds aren't the only things on the wing at this time of year. The most silent and magical migrant is the monarch butterfly. Although our garden attracts many types of butterflies—swallowtails, painted ladies, red admirals—it is the mighty (and mitey) monarch who migrates with the most ambition.

They flutter soundlessly through the yard. I don't notice one, two, or five. When I finally take note of the accumulation of butterflies, there are already hundreds. Like confetti, they float down from the sky, fluttering earthward to light on the drooping branches of a cedar tree at the top of our shade garden. And there they congregate. Tens. Then hundreds. They light, land, and close their wings to rest for the night.

In the morning the tree is cloaked in butterflies. As the sun rises, each butterfly slowly opens and closes its wings to dry off the morning dew. The tree, with hundreds of opening and closing butterflies, looks alive—as though it is inhaling and exhaling. As the sun rises higher in the sky, the butterflies flutter away until the tree stands empty. Light as a toothpick, these crepe-paper winged insects won't rest for long until they reach the Sierra Madre mountains in southern Mexico.

The exodus of our yard's songbirds reminds us that it's time to set up feeders for the birds that will tough out the winter with us. Cardinals, finches, blue jays, woodpeckers, and sparrows will entertain us, as will the occasional pheasant who wanders into the yard for the cracked corn the sloppy jays spew across the ground.

And when the cold weather settles in and the snow is piled in drifts, I'll think back on a particular bright autumn day, like today, and reconsider the message in the sky: *Go this way, Go this way.*

Frost Takes No Prisoners

Frost takes no prisoners in the garden. Sure, the parsley is still standing there stoically, and a couple of perennials can take a hit, but the annuals fold like a house of cards.

The first moments of the morning after a killing frost offer a study in contrasts. Unopened buds, ready to unfurl their fresh petals, are frozen in motion in a slim wrap of frost. Blooming roses stand glistening in the sunlight, not with dew, but crystals of ice. The perky pots of annuals on the back patio are standing straight, still in full bloom.

For about an hour, while the air is still cool, the garden looks intact, albeit under a crystal glaze of ice. But as the sun rises in the sky, the warmth sets in motion the process of decomposition. And it happens on fast forward. Within a few hours, the garden has melted into a squishy mass of tangled black stems and leaves.

Surely there is no predator of the garden more stealthy and lethal than frost. Not the nimble deer that munch the hostas down to the ground. Or the rabbits that nosh on the salad greens. Or even the blister beetles that make lace out of the Swiss chard. No footed or winged garden foe can hold a candle to the complete destruction that frost renders.

The morning after the first frost is shocking. Even though I'm usually well aware of the predicted weather, I'm always still surprised that frost has visited and, like a thief in the night, stolen the garden. Because the optimist in me (or the delusional) thinks that the golden days of summer and the dew-kissed garden will last and last and last. As silly as this sounds, I'm really more than surprised. I'm stunned—at the carnage that one small degree (that limbo line below freezing) can do.

Sometimes frost is an arbitrary executioner. It fells the front perennial border with a frigid wave, but spares the garden along the side of the garage. And it is with this cold, thumbs-up/thumbs-down decision that frost reveals the microclimates in my yard.

I've tried to put off the inevitable: Tossing a bed sheet over the salad garden; setting a glass cloche over a pot; bringing in the houseplants so they don't get nipped. But these actions don't really buy me much time—maybe a couple of days or a week. Because once the weather starts to turn, sadly, there is no amount of mulch or old blankets that will stop the changing of the seasons.

So I choose the role of observer. I watch and marvel at the casual effort with which the cold hand of frost stills the exuberance and growth of the past four months. Since May, the forward momentum of the garden has gained steam. Starting with the tiniest of seeds nestled into the cool earth and the first red shoots of peonies breaking the ground, the garden and all the plant life within it, moves like a freight train gathering speed.

June is glorious. By the end of the month, the garden has filled in. Vines are climbing upward, groundcovers are spreading sideways, and the choreography of the perennial garden is in full swing. The garden on June 30th is perfection.

But just two weeks later, fueled by summer's heat and rain, the mid-July garden is loud and unruly. By August it's bursting at the seams. And in September the rabble of the garden is overflowing the raised beds and swallowing up the paths. Then, as early as mid-month, frost stops the garden dead in its tracks. And, in effect, frost resets the calendar. This begins the slow crawl through dark winter with spring at the end of the tunnel.

Did I mention, then, how happy I am? That's because after playing a slave to the master garden (even though it is I who am a master gardener), the garden's sibilant guilty whispers have been silenced. ("Please don't suggest that you are going away this weekend—what with this green briar snaking through the shrubs?" and "I need deadheading here, please!")

And the silence is deafening. No more bouquets, no more fresh-from-the-garden salads. Just the gravedigger's job of tilling under the remains.

There are other upsides to frost—it improves the flavor of our cabbage and kales. And the dip in temperatures knocks back the insect population (the natural way!). And so the garden gets tucked in for the winter with mulch and composted manure as a blanket. And thus begins the long wait and watch for spring.

winter

Chiming In

Our house, with its ten rooms, is home to ten windup clocks that announce the time in their various ringing voices every 15 minutes.

The clocks are Doug's love and responsibility. Every day, every other day, or every week (depending on the clock) he winds them carefully. Using their individual keys, he loads them up with time that they, in turn, meticulously mete out.

And about once a month, he tries to reset them all to the same time—to no avail.

Due to the vagaries of aging windup timepieces, the clocks don't all keep time in the same way—or all ring at the same time. This may be a good thing, considering the number of clocks in the house. Instead, they have their own take on time and call out the hour, half, and quarter hours—sometimes in succession, sometimes in a bell-toned duet or trio.

It's hard to miss time passing in our house. Every fifteen minutes a crescendo of ringing ensues from all rooms.

Two clocks in our kitchen offer your choice of time. If you're running late, you can reassure yourself with the slow-running mantel clock. Or if you're eager for a guest to show up, you can check the too-fast schoolhouse clock for a sooner arrival. Graham was continuously tardy at school until he learned to depend on his cell phone for the real time—the kitchen clocks are just good-looking poseurs with hands and faces that belie the truth.

The grandfather clock in our living room punctuates time with a ringing aria at the hour. The cascading bells of the Whittington chime date back to 16th-century England. The large clock belts out its melodious tune with the last note reverberating into silence.

It seems that all the other clocks, with their lesser voices, wait until he is done before they chime in.

The upstairs mantel clock is the laggard. It finishes the concert for the hour with its regal Westminster chime—the same chime that emanates from Big Ben, the clock on London's Houses of Parliament. Our clock sounds, perhaps, a little less officious than its bigger cousin—the slow procession of notes coming from a compact, eight-inch-tall clock that sits outside our guest bedroom door. While the downstairs clocks charm visitors, the little Big Ben impersonator tortures houseguests.

"So, you really hate me..." my brother Bob says as he walks sleepily into the kitchen. He and his family were staying at our house for a visit.

"Why do you think that?" I say as I grind coffee beans.

"The clock in the hallway—it rang every 15 minutes. I didn't sleep all night," he says.

"What clock?" I say.

I wasn't gaslighting my brother. Doug, the boys, and I have lived with these quarter-hour concerts for so long that we don't hear them anymore. So we stilled the pendulums on the upstairs clocks in deference to our houseguests.

We also have two cuckoo clocks. One day, Doug decided to move the canary's cage in our bedroom to the downstairs sun porch and replace it with one of the cuckoos. Canaries don't make a peep at night. Cuckoos do. As I was just slipping into dream-inducing REM sleep at midnight, the little carved Bavarian bird came shooting out of his clock—and I about hit the ceiling. We silenced him after that, too.

For the past year, we've been clock-sitting for a friend who is out of the country. The unusual copper-clad Chelsea ship clock belonged to his grandfather and doesn't honor traditional hours, but instead measures a sailor's watch hours. The clock chimes in half-hour increments, increasing the number of bells with each half hour passing—and when 8 bells ring, the sailor's 4-hour shift is up. "Eight bells and all is well," happens six times a day at our house. And for whom does this bell toll so far from the sea?

This maritime timepiece also has a different ring—higher, brighter, louder—than the other clocks in the house. Inexplicably, I kept dreaming about San Francisco until I realized that the fast-dinging chimes sound just like a trolley bell. Mystery solved.

With so many clocks comes so much ticking. The heartbeat "tick-tock" sound can be heard everywhere in the house. I don't notice the ticking all the time, but sometimes when I sit down with a cup of coffee to relax, the slow, consistent sound is all I can hear.

It's a reassuring sound—a resonant whisper that reminds me that everything happens at its own pace: happiness, sorrow, laughter, worry, night, day, summer, winter.

It's the sound of life moving forward—slow, measured, true.

Found Objects

"This is a horse head," Brad says as he holds up a golf club. "And this," he pulls a brush out of a dusty box, "is a bird's tail."

We are wandering around a junk sale on the outskirts of Nashville, Tennessee. I'm combing through the tables of undiscovered treasure with my friends Brad and Sundie Ruppert. The Dr. Seuss-like shopping experience is due to the fact that Brad and Sundie are artists, owners of a company called Vintage, through which they make sculptures out of found objects.

You expect artists to see the world in a different way than you do, but it always amazes me how the flotsam and jetsam of a junk sale is a totally different visual experience for the Rupperts than it is for me. I see bent pieces of farm machinery—they see stork legs. I see a piece of fencing too small for any use—they see wings. I see a box full of old tablespoons—they see angels—choirs of them.

It's like going antiquing with Dr. Frankenstein.

I am a big fan of their work—and proud owner of one of their first horses. Brad made a sculpture of my quarter horse Yukon as a surprise for my birthday. The sum of Yukon's parts is an odd combo of things you might find in your basement if your basement hadn't been cleaned out for 80 years. Or your attic. Or a barn. Or a junkyard.

A golf club, a 3-iron to be precise, is Yukon's head. Two green, ribbed antique Christmas lights make his ears. His legs are cut out of ceiling tin. Because I am a writer, typewriter keys spell out his name across his body and the faces of watches indicate my deadlines. His waving mane is made from loops of 16-gauge wire. And Yukon's tail is the real deal, a tiny portion secretly snipped off by Brad and Doug while Yukon was blissfully nibbling his dinner alfalfa. Intertwined on the wires are straw-colored glass beads from Venice—purchased on a spring break trip that our families took together several years ago. (These guys save *everything*...) One of Yukon's horseshoes encircles the wooden hat-block base.

This foot-and-a-half-tall sculpture is absolutely one of my favorite things. The Rupperts liked him too, because Yukon became a prototype for a whole stable of whimsical Vintage horses. Galloping out of Brad and Sundie's imaginations, their horses are wired and studded with the things they find at auctions, flea markets, and the occasional dumpster dive. Vintage bric-a-brac from old Odd Fellows robes becomes fancy saddle blankets, and real horsehair from traditional horsehair mecates (equine lead ropes) is reconfigured as braided wind-flowing tails.

Although necessity may be the mother of invention, certainly opportunity is its second cousin. Brad and Sundie delve deep into bins, drawers, and baskets of odd parts, pulling out things no longer connected to their original use—handles, gears, cigar boxes, subway and lunch tokens. They hold them up—staring, squinting, divining a new use. And when they see a purpose, a lost article becomes found. A useless thing is employed again, completing some animal, bird, or character.

There is beauty in everything. But sometimes it takes a special eye to see the potential. Like boot jacks—the wooden v-shaped structures that cowboys use to pull off their boots. Brad and Sundie found a bunch of them at a sale. Sundie took one look and saw a dog. "It was so clear. They looked like the heads of Great Danes," she said.

Sometimes words rather than objects drive a sculpture's creation. Brad and Sundie do with language what they do with objects—bend it a little, refashioning old phrases for new use. The Lone Ranger's "Hi-Ho Silver!" inspired a Vintage horse surrounded by old tableware called "Hi-Ho Silverware."

Their studio is like a scene from a Tim Burton movie—bins of gears, boxes of game pieces (giving a home to lost dice and checkers), baskets of brushes and golf club heads, drawers of nails, studs, tokens—all their palettes of parts, connectors, and decorative embellishments. The bins of other people's castoffs and the machinery-parts menagerie validate the old saying, "One man's trash is another man's treasure." And if not treasure, at least a torso or a head.

So now when I go to antique shops, flea markets or auctions, I linger over boxes of random stuff that has been collected together by happenstance or default and think, "What would Brad and Sundie see in this?" What disconnected pieces are waiting to rise out of the rust like a fantastically decorated phoenix?

Short but Fulfilling Winter Days

The alarm goes off and I crack open an eye. It can't possibly be morning because it's still inky black outside, so I hit the snooze, turn over in denial, and fall blissfully back to sleep. Ten minutes later my alarm confirms the bad news—it is indeed morning and I reluctantly get up and dress.

Doug and I divvy up the morning chores by species. My wards are the barn inhabitants—horses, donkeys, and sheep. His charges are everyone else—our turbocharged dogs, hungry farm cats, a flock of egg-laying chickens, and a cage of cooing white doves. We pull on layers of clothes until we resemble Mr. and Mrs. Michelin Man and head out the door in different directions.

As I step off the back porch, the wind hits me full force in the face. I breathe in deeply and my nostrils freeze together. Not a good sign. I walk past the outdoor thermometer, but don't bother to squint in the darkness for a temperature reading. It can't tell me anything that my Wellingtons squeaking on the hard snow haven't told me already. It's cold. Really cold. Snap, our intrepid Jack Russell terrier, runs beside me on three legs—final confirmation that it's too cold for man or beast.

Although the barn isn't far from the house, the weather conditions dictate how long it will take me to get there. If it has snowed, there may be thigh-high drifts to negotiate. On icy days, a trip to the barn resembles the Monty Python "Ministry of Silly Walks" segment.

Inside the barn it's like Grand Central Station. Crowded together, the animals exhibit the same level of tolerance that busy train riders afford each other—lots of bodies crammed into a small area trying not to invade the personal spaces of others. These days we have a dozen sheep, four donkeys, and three horses, all of whom expect to be fed at the same time every morning and evening. It's not so much to ask, but they're a tough crowd when I'm running late. Lots of bumping and grumbling. I always apologize out loud: "I needed to make coffee," I offer. "I hit the snooze twice," I confess. No absolution here.

In winter, the radio plays 24/7 to brighten their short days. Our breakfast soundtrack this morning is a baroque tune—a greatest hit from a previous century. Hay and grain quickly quell all movement except chewing, and I pause a moment to listen to the animals munching their food in a symphony of satisfaction. Outside, the wind whips up again, styling the snow on the ground into sugarcoated swirls against the woven wire fence.

I trudge back toward the house and watch lights in the second story click on. I look up to see our kids lumber from room to room getting ready for school, checking their email, and neglecting, once again, to make their beds.

Elsewhere on the farm, life is moving faster. Doug feeds our three black-and-white Border collies: Rose, Floss, and Tweed. After they wolf down their food, they zip around the yard like shadow and light across the snow. Alba, our Great Pyrenees, lumbers like a polar bear across the snow, failing to keep up with the trio of fleet Border collies, a big smile on her face nonetheless.

Doug feeds and waters the chickens, but he'll collect no eggs today because in weather this cold they're frozen solid about an hour after the chickens lay them. Maybe later today I'll head out to the chicken house and collect the cracked frozen eggs, thaw them out, and make scrambled eggs for the barn cats. It's a good use of ruined eggs, and there's something comic and satisfying about serving up a steaming pan of eggs to our crew of farm cats.

All of the morning's hubbub comes to an abrupt halt at 8 a.m. when my sons and husband head off to school and work, respectively. My commute to work is much shorter. I step from my dining room into my office, sit down in front of my computer, and open my emails from the night before. Thanks to my speedy DSL line, the world is at my fingertips. My brother Bob, who lives in Sweden, has a funny story about the antics of his baby son Noah. My friend Peter, in Tokyo, is starting a business selling Japanese prints and wants me to check out his new website. My niece Oksana wants me to buy wrapping paper for her third-grade fundraiser. I answer emails, then get to work—conjuring up from memory the scent and sight of roses for an article I'm writing about growing them. I look up from my computer screen and watch, for a moment, the snow-dusted horses milling about the barnyard, nibbling at morsels of hay. I write for a little longer then hit a blank wall on what to say next, and determine it's time for a second cup of coffee.

Today, like most days, is a good one—filled with the things I love the most: my family, the soft eyes of animals, and the exchanged missives from friends far away. Outside the wind is kicking up again. But inside this old house—that creaks with each stiff gale—I feel like I am riding on a big ship, traveling to an unknown destination, confident that we're headed the right way.

Snow Day!

Reading Willa Cather, Ole Rölvaag, and other writers of 19th-century American rural life, it's apparent that winter was a whole different experience 100 years ago. A winter storm for a prairie family presented a life and death situation. Food and medical supply lines drifted shut, contact with the outside world closed down, and the howling wind and snow leveled the landscape.

Yet in our century-old farmhouse, a bad snowstorm means just one thing: the spontaneous possibility of that most beloved of all holidays—the snow day. A snow day is an arbitrary holiday—a day merely borrowed from the school calendar and reinstated at the end of the year. But my kids are giddy with excitement over the roulette wheel that winter spins, and its ability to buy them a day of freedom.

When the first snowflake appears, my youngest son looks expectantly out the window and asks, "Do you think the road will drift shut?" Looking out the window and seeing no more flakes, I answer, "Not unless that snow flake has lots of friends." And he sighs sadly, making a cloud of breath against the window.

On some winter mornings, however, my kids' wildest dreams are realized. We all wake to a still white world. The dark edges of the winter landscape are smoothed and softened with pounds of snow. Beyond the house, large undefined shapes mark where our cars were parked in the driveway, no longer distinguishable from the rest of the yard. Swooping drifts of snow rise and fall across the road like suspended waves on the ocean. The trees wear heavy cloaks of sparkling snow. Not a single track mars the seamless surface. The land is soundless, motionless. We're snowed in!

The first order of the morning is staying warm. This is a basic knee jerk reaction I know I share with the prairie women of a century ago. The big difference is that our neatly stacked wood outdoors feeds a fireplace that provides as much ambience as it does warmth. The real heat in the house comes from the efficient furnace humming along with purpose in the basement. Nevertheless, on a frigid day like today you need a fire.

As it happens, the firewood box is empty because, in this century, a surprise snowstorm is a treat, not a tragedy. We haven't planned ahead. So we send the kids outdoors to unbury the sled and fetch a load of wood. As they suit up for the cold, Doug switches on the TV to learn the story of the snowstorm—who it has stranded on the highway and what it will do next. We hear that traffic is at a standstill on the Interstate, snowplows are clearing the main routes, and that, "If you don't need to go out, stay home." The kids pound on the door with their load of wood, then stomp into the house, pulling off their hats and mittens, which spew tiny snowballs everywhere. Their eyes lock onto the television. When the newsman finally utters the magical words, "SNOW DAY," great cheers of glee ring throughout the house.

The kids jump back into their pajamas and start in on making the best of their free day—they turn on their computers to play video games. Doug and I exchange shrugs and start a fire. We're snowed in too, but we know how to spend this day. We'll have a luxurious day off in a way that our 19th-century forebears could not. We keep the fire well stoked and watch old movies on TV. Later in the day I mix up a batch of cookie dough, and the smell of baking chocolate chips gently lures our sons downstairs to the kitchen where we'll all sit in the same warm room to celebrate the snow day in style.

Although we own a tractor with a blade *and* a snow blower (not to mention lots of shovels), on snow days we don't budge from the house. It's like the snowstorm has issued us all "Get Out of Jail Free" cards and we happily chuck responsibilities for the day. Digging out can wait until tomorrow.

Straw into Gold

"If you swear again, you'll have to leave the class." The instructor's voice was firm, authoritative, and mirthless.

I was sitting in an adult education, Scandinavian wheat weaving class. My goal was to weave straw into cute little holiday ornaments and stocking stuffers.

As I was struggling with a stiff strand of wheat, I wondered who the instructor was censuring. I glanced up and her eyes were directed, like missiles, at me. I straightened up in my chair and smiled warmly at her. "Did I say something?" I asked.

"Yes!" she glared. "You just shouted ____," and she repeated a swear word that did, in fact, sound familiar.

I apologized. Who knew that the frustration fest heating up inside my head had vented into the open air of the classroom?

This wheat-weaving business would have brought down even the likes of Rumpelstiltskin, the fictional dwarf in the Grimm Brothers' fairy tale who could spin straw into gold. I sat with my pile of wheat straw heaped in an unruly mess in front of me and felt like the entrapped miller's daughter of the story. Straw into gold? Wheat into ornaments? I don't think so...

The class was comprised of a dozen women who gathered once a week at night in a high school chemistry lab to spin wheat into gold. Hunched over our little haystacks, working around the gas outlets and the lab sinks, we would cut wheat shafts, soak them in water, then deftly braid them into elaborate honey-colored hearts, wreaths, ornaments, and centerpieces.

Or at least that was what the course description promised...

My wheat wasn't cooperating. Just as I was finishing a neatly braided strip, one of the pieces snapped off in my hand, spewing a shower of golden wheat seeds all over the floor—and another colorful word into the room.

I coughed loudly, trying to cover myself, and avoided the wincing eyes of the instructor (who I could easily imagine as the figurehead on a Viking warship).

Wheat ornaments are standard holiday decorations in Scandinavia. I returned from a holiday visit to Sweden to see my brother Bob and his family with my suitcase filled with a small herd of wheat reindeer that I bought in a Gothenberg grocery store. And you can't step a booted foot into an Ikea during the winter months without being greeted by hundreds of wheaten animals, wreaths, and elves created from this versatile grain.

There was something about weaving the wheat myself that I found appealing. But as many of my crafting adventures had turned out, this one was harder than it looked. I'm kind of an instant-gratification crafter, and wheat weaving was proving to involve both a skill and patience that I didn't have.

"You've done this before, right?" I ask the woman sitting next to me, whose hands resembled a wheat-weaving machine working at top speed.

"No, I haven't, but it's really fun and relaxing, isn't it?" she said, neither looking up nor breaking her rapid weaving pace.

I felt a sharp twinge of pain over my right eye. "Oh yes," I said smiling. "I'm just having a blast." I enviously eyed the expanding pile of little wheat shapes in front of her. Thoughtful, handmade ornaments for everyone in her family and neighborhood, no doubt. Maybe even her whole town.

But although I might shout curses in inappropriate situations, I was no quitter. I attended every class and learned how to weave wheat. And at the end of the class, I had three tiny, tortured wheat weavings that looked more like wind-tossed bird nests than holiday decorations. I hung them proudly on my kitchen door, and I rarely corrected any visitors who gushed over my "kids' cute little straw things." (Luckily my children were too young at the time to be insulted by association with such shoddy craftsmanship.)

But most importantly, I learned a new skill that I can use in any season, any situation—the ability to curse under my breath without anyone hearing me.

Closet Confessions

Our century-old farmhouse is a simple design. Called a foursquare, it features four rooms on the bottom floor and four rooms on the top. In the original floor plan of the house, there was one closet. Just one.

And so I became enamored with the concept of the armoire.

The armoire is the George Clooney of furniture—it's both cute and smart. Essentially a big freestanding closet, the armoire dates to the 16th century where it was originally built to store arms and armor (the word we use today is from the French version of the Latin *armârium* which means chest, and *arma* which means tools).

When I bought my first armoire I was smitten. It was a hulking, double-doored cupboard made of oak. When we got it home from the antique store, Doug and I had an unpleasant epiphany. The armoire barely fit through the front door and was too monstrous to take up the stairs to our second floor bedroom. After much whining, hand wringing, and a modicum of swearing, we removed the ornately carved crown, hoisted the decapitated cabinet up the stairs, then repositioned the top piece. No harm done. But that piece of furniture is there to stay. Forever.

I now have ten armoires.

Four armoires reside in our bedrooms, serving as the closets the house didn't originally provide. A seven-foot-tall armoire sits in the corner of our kitchen as an entertainment center. The green-painted doors close off the television from view and serve as a reminder to me that there are more important things than watching *House* reruns.

If one were to open up the discreet doors of my armoires, the truth about me would be revealed—that I find folding clothes and linens a somewhat tedious job and often resort to the stash-and-run theory of home organization.

Many of my armoires hint at secret pasts—of centuries and countries I'll never live in. But that doesn't stop me from filling in details of stories I'll never know the truth about...

For example, the white pine armoire in our living room came from Belgium. It's called a maid's chest and although it's nearly seven feet tall, it disassembles into pieces small enough to travel with. In my case, it traveled from an antique store in Galena, Illinois, to my home via the back of my station wagon. When we got home, Doug and I reassembled it like a puzzle. How many households had this armoire traveled to? Who brought it to the United States? I imagine Dutch painter Johannes Vermeer's *Girl with a Pearl Earring* as a previous owner...

Without a closet on the main level of our house, we added an armoire to the foyer as a coat closet. The Arts and Crafts wardrobe that stows our winter wraps was built in England. The nameplate on the inside of the mirrored door reads: A.E. Clare, House Furnishings, 364, Moseley Rd., Birmingham. (A quick search on Google revealed that this address is now home to an auto parts store.) A hint of a past owner is revealed every time I open the door—the unmistakable scent of pipe smoke materializes like a spirit. I envision a Sherlock-Holmes-type character wearing a tweed deerstalker hat with billows of blue pipe smoke encircling his head. Sometimes I'll stand with my head in the armoire for a long moment and breathe deeply, thinking about C.S. Lewis' wonderful children's novel *The Lion, the Witch and the Wardrobe,* and wondering what sort of fantasy world lies just beyond our coats.

The armoire in Tristan's bedroom was employed as a canning cupboard in a previous life, and still bears witness to the success of a past harvest-and-canning season. Handwritten in chalk on the upper inside of the left-hand door is the following list: 7 qt. dill pickle, 9 qt. apricots, 6 qt. peaches. I see a plain, hardy woman—one that Grant Wood might have painted—in a floral-print housedress, and I imagine the gentle clinking of Ball jars as she stocks the cabinet with her garden's bounty.

Although my house is full (and, thanks to armoires, fairly organized), I can't seem to stop coveting these great pieces of furniture. At auctions, in antique stores, at tag sales, I'm drawn to their large-shouldered, reassuring shapes. In fact, I've never met an armoire I didn't like. So efficient, so useful, so handsome—with wide-open arms, willing to take in all the accumulations of my life.

Faux, Faux, Faux…Merry Christmas!

One of my earliest Christmas memories is of the aluminum foil tree that lit up the living room of my grandparents' home. It twirled slowly, played festive holiday music, and changed color like a chameleon—blue, red, yellow. It was glittery, electric, and bright. But even as a four-year-old child, I considered this tree to be a poser, a wannabe, a fake. How could a Christmas tree be anything other than a real tree?

A real tree is what we had at home. My memories of the Christmas trees of my childhood are a virtual forest of short, squat pines that were purchased from one of the tree lots that sprouted up in vacant parking lots in the early days of December. Fresh, fragrant, and prickly as porcupines, the holiday trees of my childhood were usually as wide as they were tall.

Every year there was some decorating debacle. One year we draped "angel hair" over the branches. This spun-glass decoration made the tree look snowy and ephemeral, but caused painful red rashes on any skin that came in contact with the stuff. The next year our insatiable Cocker Spaniel Muffy ate all the ornaments off the bottom of the tree. Then there was the year my sister Susie was a toddler, and my mother erected the tree, fully decorated, in a wooden playpen. Caged and safe from the prying fingers of children, the tree glowed from the center of the living room while my brother, sister, and I stood at its edges staring through the wooden bars at our gifts.

One holiday when I returned home from college, I discovered that my mother had abandoned the fresh-cut for the fake. Her first faux tree was little better than green bottlebrushes wedged into a brown broomstick. (Faux tree technology was to improve greatly in ensuing years.) It was sparse and far too symmetrical to come close to successfully imitating a real tree. For this tree (and the better-looking one she got later), my mother braved family ridicule from her four tree-snob children, and, to her credit, never once attempted to poison our eggnog in retaliation.

So when it came to my first Christmas as a tree buyer, it was going to be the real thing. Doug and I traveled to a nearby Christmas tree farm. Located in a beautiful river valley, it could have easily served as a backdrop for a Currier and Ives print. We trudged up and down the snow-covered hills, sizing up trees until we spotted the perfect one.

In its happy little grove on a hill, the pine looked comfortable and in scale. Yet when we dragged it up on the front porch, it took on the appearance of a menacing bear. Getting it into the house was a tug of war that we won only with a dramatic spray of needles all over the rug. Undaunted, we whittled down the thick trunk. (Why didn't we think about doing this outdoors?) until finally it looked like a sharpened pencil tip that was slender enough to fit into our antique tree stand. The tree wavered dangerously as we placed the angel on top. Immediately our two cats tried to climb the trunk, sending the angel flying. After they felled the tree twice in the same week, we wired it to the staircase so tightly it would have taken cougars to tip it.

On his first Christmas, we bundled up Tristan for his maiden voyage to the tree farm. When I look at photos of that day, I'm shocked at what they reveal. Our four-month-old baby was swaddled in blankets and wedged into a sleigh with a bow saw as big as he was. In hindsight, dragging a baby through the woods with a saw as his traveling companion seemed to be poor judgment, but we were new parents and we had a tree to cut down.

Subsequent years of holiday photographs show squat, shrubby trees held upright by guy wires and sparsely dotted with clinging ornaments. Yet nothing could persuade us that this Christmas tradition was anything but lovely.

Then last year things changed. We had scheduled a trip out of town a week before the holidays. The prospect of a dry, sap-filled tree draped in electrical wires seemed foolhardy. (My paranoid side always presents itself in headlines: "Twinkle-Light Tragedy Torches 100-Year-Old House".)

So we went safely faux. We got a nice "Douglas fir" with white lights embedded in the branches—try that one, Mother Nature! As we unpacked the tree from the car, I shuddered to think what my mother was going to say. (She showed incredible self-restraint.)

And so, although I live in the country surrounded by the gentle forms of snow-covered conifers, I've come to accept that my perfect holiday tree is artificial. But that, of course, doesn't make the events that happen around it any less real.

Every Picture Tells a Story

The winter snowstorm raging outside my window brings an unexpected gift—a day of weather-related confinement at home in front of my fireplace. Yet being snowed in makes me restless, so I start the long-overdue project of sifting through the hundreds of loose photographs in the green wooden trunk at the foot of my bed.

These photos—Doug and I sunburned on a beach, our sons hamming it up at a miniature golf course, gap-toothed school pictures, family pets, birthday parties, holiday dinners—are the documentation of our life. As I lay the photos out on the floor, I wonder what sort of story they tell.

I've done this before, piecing together a story from a trunk of photos brought down from the attic of my grandparents' house following the death of my grandfather. My mother, sisters, grandmother, and I began the sorting. As we opened the albums and boxes of loose photos, the dry odor of history rose from black-and-white and sepia-toned prints. We organized the photos into two stacks: people we knew and people we didn't. The people-we-didn't-know pile was large and interesting.

"Who is this?" I said, holding up a black-and-white photo of an elegantly dressed woman wearing a hat the size of a dinner platter.

My grandmother studied it and said, "I have no idea."

"Do you know who this is?" I said as I held up another photo.

"I have no clue," she said, continuing to rifle through photos.

With each photo's lack of identification, I felt another door in the long corridor of our family history quietly close and lock tight.

I pulled out a photo of a small boy and a tall woman standing in front of a train car—not a passenger train, but a freight train. The boxcar was not perched upon tracks, but was sitting in the middle of a field of grass.

"Who are these people?" I asked.

My grandmother's faced brightened with recognition. "Oh, that's your grandfather and his mother when they lived in a train car."

What? A train car?

"So what's the story here?" I asked excitedly.

My grandmother looked up and said. "No story. He just lived in a train car when he was little."

Stop right there. We are a family of storytellers. Our family's oral history involves a dozen or so well-told (and well-worn) anecdotes. These stories, told ad nauseam at family gatherings, created the architecture of my life. It's how I knew not to challenge my mother to a swimming race; family history had her stroking with ease across Lake Loon and back. It's what kept me from baiting my grandfather into a fight; his first job was as a coyote bounty hunter. And how I knew that my grandmother would wipe the floor with me at basketball; she had an album of newspaper clippings of her on-court exploits when she and her two sisters played on a women's league in Chicago.

On my mother's side of the family the stories range from the embarrassing to the amazing. My great-grandfather Oscar was a sheriff who challenged every man he arrested to a fight, with the chance to win back his freedom. The family story goes that he never had to release a single arrestee, and chewed off one poor fellow's ear in the deal.

Ding, ding, ding! A new family story was like winning the genealogical jackpot.

But if the story of a comforter, the one that my mother and her two sisters actually *named* "Big Fluff", was the most-told family story, then shouldn't the "living in a train car" story have made it into the top ten? Perhaps with so many nuts in the family tree, "living in a train car" just didn't make the cut. I shuddered to think what other stories remained untold.

Selective, collective memory. Family historians winnow through the memories both good and bad, sifting, editing, retouching, until the stories are just right. Then these tales are told and repeated until they wear the fine patina of truth. Everything else goes into the trunk.

As I shuffle through the photographic flotsam and jetsam of my own immediate family, I wonder what these family photos will reveal about us. Who is this Jack Russell terrier wearing a red fez? Why are these two young boys whacking each other with sticks in the center of a Roman coliseum? What was so funny all the time?

Tracking Movements

My favorite type of snowstorm is one that blows in under the cloak of darkness, then drops giant doily-like flakes all night long. No wind, just a silent snowy deluge that's expended by dawn. I love to wake up to the landscape entirely erased by snow—smooth, flawless, and undulating beneath a blanket of white.

After a newly fallen snow, I'm always amazed at the number of animal tracks that zigzag across our yard. It seems that during the day I can stare out the window for hours and never catch a single trespasser. But at night our yard is a hub of activity. Or so the tracks—hoof, paw, and claw—reveal on a newly fallen snow.

Distinctive almond-shaped, double hoof-prints of deer travel down our gravel road and dip into the shallow ditch in front of our house. They then disappear for eight or ten feet—indicating an effortless leap over our perennial garden and four-foot-tall fence—and reappear with a slight slide into the front yard. And there they stand, sunken slightly into the frozen lawn, just feet from the steps of our front porch. If I were awake at 4 a.m., would I see this antlered buck flying into our front yard like Donder or Blitzen? And does he pause there in front of the picture window, tilting his heavy head in curiosity at the placement of a conifer tree (our bejeweled and twinkling Christmas tree) inside the house?

The yard's tracks tell stories of other midnight activity. For example, the rabbit population in our area must congregate in our side yard for a clandestine meeting after a new snow. The pogo-stick front feet and flat back feet of rabbit tracks meander here, then there. Tracks wander to the leafless shrubbery where the branch tips of viburnums and dogwoods serve up succulent treats. Then the hopping prints appear to form a conga line, cha-cha-cha-ing across the lawn, into the woods, through the woven wire fence, and into the pasture beyond. The rabbits leave their footprints dotted with occasional punctuation marks of dark droppings in the snow.

Footprints of our barn cats are signs of more purposeful movement. They emanate from the barn and garage where hay bales, old comforters, and heat lamps make snug bedding through the winter for them. The little round tracks of soft cat feet make a beeline directly to the back patio of our house, where breakfast and dinner are served regardless of the weather.

Tracks from our dogs' morning run tell a different story. The paw prints weave and bound all over the yard showing clear interest in the scents and signs of deer, rabbits, and who knows what else. The canine steps—from our Great Pyrenees Alba's round saucer-sized print to the tippy-tap-dancing footprints of the Jack Russells, Snap and Archer—show a sense of exuberance and a lack of attention span as they swoop under the bushes, toward the bird feeders, and into the garage to nose the cats in their warm beds.

In the barnyard, tracks crisscross the paddock with hints to which animals actually enjoy the snow, and who in the barn just tolerate it. The sheep, although clad in thick wool coats, don't seem to relish the new snowfall as evidenced by their reluctant, to-the-point tracks. Apparently, one sheep blazes a trail from the barn through the snow to the hay feeder and all the subsequent sheep follow in the same path. Is it out of respect for the first brave "explorer" sheep? Or could it be a wise necessity, not wanting to expend extra energy in the coldest of months? The horse tracks are more creative. Widely spaced hoofprints indicate speed and playfulness as the tracks gallop back and forth across the paddock.

Under the bird feeders, tiny trident-shape prints of juncos and sparrows are mere whispers on the snow.

And the final tracks, ours, Doug's and mine, tell the tale of a typical snowy morning: a path leading to the barn for morning chores and a trail through the drifts to the bird feeders to pack them with sunflower seeds for the cardinals and jays, thistle seed for the finches, and suet for the woodpeckers. Then quick steps, sometimes bounds, back to the house for a steaming cup of coffee.

By midday, as the sun rises higher in the sky, the precise tracks melt into soft white smudges—a visual echo of the hustle and flow every night beneath our darkened windows.

Life of Riley

"Don't you think this scarf would look good on Riley?" I asked Tristan and Graham as we loaded up our holiday shopping cart.

They exchanged looks.

"No. Please. No," they said in unison. They knew if I was accessory shopping for our miniature donkey Riley, then I must be contemplating our family Christmas card photo.

For the past several years, we'd tried taking our holiday card photos with a variety of animals on our farm.

One year we decked the necks of our draft horses, Ben and Sam, with live fir wreaths. Because the wreaths were round and heavy like harness collars, they didn't think twice as we slipped them over their heads. The greens looked festive encircling their broad blonde necks. But while we were setting up the shot, posing our sons, getting the background just right, Sam realized Ben's "collar" was edible and he reached over and pulled off a big mouthful of fir bough. Ben reciprocated, munching a giant chunk out of Sam's wreath. Tristan and Graham pulled with all of their might to keep the horses apart as I shot two rolls of film.

The finished photos told the story. Struggling boys. Straining horses. Stripped wreaths. Not a single pair of eyes was looking at the camera. And no one was smiling.

We sent cards without photos that year.

"But this year," I thought hopefully, "if the equines were smaller and their neckwear less edible…"

I had picked out sweaters from Doug's side of our armoire for the kids to wear.

"I'm *not* going to wear *that*," Tristan said, as he looked disdainfully at the sweater in my hand.

"It's just a prop," I said. "Sweaters are warm, happy, and festive. Put it on," I urged, bracing myself for a row.

When my sons were younger, they would comply with the odd costume request happily. But now that they were teenagers, they were more likely to roll their eyes, shake their heads, and try to leave the room unnoticed.

While we were arguing about the sweater, I realized that the whole point was moot. The photo I envisioned just wouldn't work. Riley was a miniature donkey (the operative word being miniature) and measured just 36 inches at the shoulder. Both Tristan and Graham were 6 foot 2 inches tall. A close-up group photo of them together would result in a strange shot of the tips of Riley's ears and the torsos of my sons. Not really holiday card material. I rethought my plan.

I'm not sure how animals perceive color, but when I walked out to the pasture with a red scarf in my hand, it caused quite a stir. The horses galloped around me and the sheep skittered into flock formation. But Riley walked up right to me. He seemed to say, "My, what an attractive scarf." (Could it be that I've watched too many Disney films in my life?) I held it out to him. No complaints, no alternative color suggestions, no shrugging and walking away. He simply stepped right up and I tied the scarf jauntily around his neck.

Red was definitely Riley's color.

As I stood in the pasture with a donkey wearing a red scarf, I thought back on the long tradition of dressing up pets for photos. William Wegman draped his elegant Weimaraner, Fay Ray, in canine couture for a multitude of amazing photos. And who doesn't think chimps look great in clothes—especially formalwear? At the holidays, every pet store sells antler headbands to put on cats (who really hate it) and dogs (who are fairly oblivious to it).

As you might expect, donkeys aren't sartorially savvy and Riley leaned down and nibbled the scarf's fringe. "Must all our pets eat their costumes?" I thought with great exasperation as I adjusted the scarf's loose ends to rest on the top of his neck. Now he resembled a large, elaborately wrapped gift. I took a dozen snapshots of him from all sides while he stood there benignly posing.

When I picked up the prints at the one-hour photo shop, I excitedly opened the envelope. As I shuffled through them, I became acutely aware that I was standing in a public place with a handful of photos of a barnyard animal wearing clothing. I hastily stuffed them back into the envelope.

Without the photography skills of William Wegman (or the fashionable togs of Fay Ray), my attempt at pet posing was clownish at best. Disturbing at worst.

Perhaps we would send cards without photos again this year.

Here's the funny thing, though. It turns out that Riley likes to wear the scarf. So as I sit down to address holiday cards, a smallish chocolate-colored donkey calmly munches alfalfa hay by the barn, his red scarf fluttering in the breeze.

Star Power

The sun goes down much earlier than it should in winter, and the landscape fades to black. If this were a movie, you would expect something to happen next. But the sunrise is a good ten hours away—and the distance between the dark and the dawn allows ample time to study the drama of the night sky.

If the sky is cloudless, the heavens above you feel large and expansive, as if you're standing in the middle of outer space. If there's a full moon, it shines down on you like a spotlight, lighting up the flat, snowy landscape and performing a nighttime sleight of hand that allows you to cast a shadow in the middle of the night. And once the moon has traveled to the other side of the world, the dark night sky rewards you with the thrill of a little celestial bling—a dizzying array of stars studding the night like a wild toss of diamonds onto black velvet.

In winter, the Big Dipper tips and ladles darkness over our house as Doug and I walk down the road, taking the dogs for their last run of the day. Where we live in the country there is little light pollution, so the sky is inky, liquid black. Overhead, the Milky Way glows.

I stop and focus on the glittering dots in the sky and notice, after a moment, the slow-moving ones that aren't stars, but jets. High in the heavens they cross the sky at 30,000 feet, going from coast to coast. Blinking blips from my gravel-road vantage point, they crawl slowly from Orion to Canis Major and beyond. I imagine for a moment that a blanket-wrapped passenger looks away from her movie and gazes out her window into darkness below, but she doesn't see us or our darting dogs on this dark country road, making our footprint trails through the snow in this silent, fly-over land.

On a good night, there is a falling star. And I never fail to make a wish. I remember seeing my first falling star at summer camp when I was eight. We were sleeping under the stars, but I wasn't sleeping. Instead, I was staring up into the nothingness, amazed that this was the same sky I had at home, when I spied movement out of the corner of my eye. I turned my head on my pillow to watch a star speeding across the silent sky. I wasn't fast enough to call out to my fellow campers, and no one saw it but me. My own falling star.

What could possibly be more fantastic than a star falling from the sky? It's still a thrill to catch that moment, that you—and perhaps a handful of others in the world who happen to be staring up into the sky at that exact split second—witness the soundless arc of light, the quick flash into darkness. It seems like you should do something with this experience. But what?

The grand dame of the night sky is a meteor shower—like the fireworks finale on the Fourth of July. Winter meteor shows include the Leonid, Geminid, and Quadrantid. But it's a cold proposition to lie in your snowy front yard at 2:30 a.m., looking upward into the heavens waiting for the star show to begin. I've given it a whirl, but after an uncomfortably cold half hour with nary a blink in the sky, I decided that the Leonid would most likely be just the colder (but not cooler) sequel of the Perseid, one of the summertime meteor showers. Call me a wimp, but I want my falling stars in warm weather.

On the seemingly endless nights of winter like these, it's not hard to feel like a bit player in a great drama. Billions of stars blazing brightly above, constellations changing position, jets so high up that they're mere blinks, meteor showers that etch the sky with dying light. But in the darkness of the winter night, the distance between the stars and the Earth seems somehow closer—a celestial ceiling and the snow-covered ground, with so much dark mystery in between.

Regarding Winter

One must have a mind of winter / To regard the frost and the boughs / Of the pine-trees crusted with snow; / And have been cold a long time / To behold the junipers shagged with ice, / The spruces rough in the distant glitter / Of the January sun...

These lines are from one of my favorite poems "The Snowman," by Wallace Stevens. Although I have an increasingly hard time remembering important things like my cell phone number, I have this poem committed to memory. And when I'm walking to the barn in the blue light of morning to feed the horses or trudging behind running dogs in the pasture with the cold air grabbing for my breath, it's these lines that whisper continually in my mind.

Because I have a mind of winter.

One doesn't have to read many man-against-nature novels—Jack London comes to mind—or mountain climbing accounts such as *Into Thin Air* to know that Snow Is Not Your Friend. (This also includes Snow's slickster cousins Ice and Sleet.)

I didn't have to be drifted into a mountain pass for three months or slip into an icy abyss to discover this fact. The dark side of snow revealed itself to me as I was standing on the flat and solid ground of my gravel road, retrieving my mail, when my feet shot out from under me and I landed squarely on my back. As I lie there staring up into the bright and cloudless sky, I began to contemplate winter's insidiousness. It is snow, and its slippery ways, that elevates simple household tasks such as mail retrieval to the same danger level as mountain climbing.

But what I love about this poem is the suggestion that winter's long occupation of the landscape will somehow reveal something—something important, something useful. And having been cold a long time—living, working, and walking through the woods and fields crystallized into stillness by the cold—I feel like I am waiting for a revelation. And so winter delivers odd and memorable epiphanies:

Glimpses of the sublime. Snow falls for hours, dropping straight down from the sky with a beautiful steadiness. So much movement, but no sound. When it stops, the outbuildings, trees, and ground are softened, blurred. The pasture stretches as far as the horizon–all blemishes of stone, stump, or footprint erased, and for this moment, the land looks new, undiscovered, and expectant.

Brushes with the bizarre. After a particularly heavy snowstorm accompanied by high winds, our yard was decorated with finely sculpted snow banks that resembled cresting waves—right down to the little curl at the top. Although our farm is landlocked for thousands of miles in all directions, the storm had delivered white-capped swells to the prairie. It didn't take the barn cats long to realize that the waves were the highest and sunniest spots in the yard so they each curled up on a crest for an afternoon snooze—creating the bizarre illusion of a row of sleeping, surfing kitties.

The need for diversion. One storm started as rain, graduated to sleet, then settled into a hard pounding of ice. I woke in the morning to find our farmyard encased in a magical, glittery, hard-candy coating. Enchanted, I stepped out the back door and did a pratfall on the porch. Crawling back to the door on my knees, I decided it was a good day to stay indoors. So I settled onto the couch with a steaming cup of tea and watched our sheep performing their version of the Ice Follies. (Even sure-footed quadrupeds fall down on ice.) After an hour of watching livestock pinballing around the paddock, I conceded that my kids were right. It was time to get satellite television. Now we can tune into more than 100 channels. And if a program featuring ice or snow flickers across the screen, we can make it go away with the click of a remote button.

A sense of humility. Winter has confirmed my antlike significance in this landscape. I live here, work here, but I am not in charge. To solidify this point, one storm took out the power at our farm for several days. The ice felled a series of Atlas-sized towers that connected electrical lines across our county—you could see them for miles, one after another, bent at the knees by the will and weight of ice. And although we dragged split logs to the house on sleds, stoked the fireplace to a comfortable blaze, and amused ourselves by reading and doing homework by oil lamp, we felt small and humbled as the long shadows of afternoon faded into the inky night.

And so each winter I endure the cold temperatures, tolerate the wicked wind that whips across the prairie with impersonal persistence, and I try to discover something new. But I'm always leaning forward a bit, tilting my head to listen for the imperceptible sounds of the world beneath the snow slowly awakening into life again.

About Karen Weir-Jimerson

Karen Weir-Jimerson lives and gardens on three acres in Woodward, Iowa. She and her husband, Doug, renovated a 1903 foursquare farmhouse where they live with a small menagerie of livestock and pets: horses, donkeys, sheep, birds, dogs, and cats.

Karen has a BA in English from the University of Iowa where she was a participant in the Writer's Workshop Undergraduate program in poetry. She graduated with a MA in English from the University of South Carolina where she did her thesis under the direction of James Dickey.

Karen currently writes the "Slow Lane" column for *Country Gardens* magazine. She is former columnist for *Country Home* magazine and has written numerous books on gardening, which include *Better Homes and Gardens From Garden to Plate* and *Better Homes and Gardens Herb Gardening*.

Read more about Karen Weir-Jimerson at:
www.karenweirjimerson.com
www.somuchsky.com

CPSIA information can be obtained at www.ICGtesting.com
Printed in the USA
LVOW061107150512

281814LV00003B/122/P